MW00935753

Creating Space

to Thrive

Get Unstuck, Reboot Your

Creativity and Change Your

Life

Courtney Kenney

First Edition
Copyright © 2017 Courtney Kenney

Also by Courtney Kenney

Layoff Reboot: Bounce Back from Job Loss and Find a Career You Love

Unleash Your Author: Write a Book in 30 Days

7-Step Book Launch Plan: Strategies to Publish and Promote Your Book

This book is for Steve.

Thanks for challenging me to live a full life.

Contents

Free Bonus Content for You

Your copy of this book includes free bonuses, so you can get started on your creative reboot, and be on your way to feeling happier and less stressed.

Because I want you to get the most value from this book, I am giving you a FREE workbook to accompany this book. It contains room for you to answer important questions as you read.

I'm passionate about adding more creativity into our lives, so I am also sharing my favorite creativity tips by giving you my book, *21 Creativity Hacks: A To-Do List for Your Inner Creative* for free.

You'll be able to download the books to the device of your choice or print out a PDF if you prefer. These books are over $10 in value and are yours for free, so grab your copies today!

Claim your free gifts by visiting: projectmanagerwriter.com/thrivebonus.

Part One: Discover Your Creativity

"There is no way that this winter is ever going to end as long as this groundhog keeps seeing his shadow. I don't see any other way out. He's got to be stopped. And I have to stop him."

-Bill Murray as Phil Connors in the 1993 movie *Groundhog Day*

Is Something Missing?

Bill Murray's character in the 1993 movie *Groundhog Day* is forced to live the same day over and over. He tries everything to change his situation, including kidnapping the town's main attraction, Punxsutawney Phil.

Unless you're a weather reporter, you probably won't find yourself assigned to a small town in Pennsylvania to report on the annual Groundhog Day festivities. But the movie serves as an allegory for self-improvement. Murray's character can't escape the loop until he finally puts the needs of others above his own.

The movie resonates with me because I felt stuck on repeat for so long. Maybe others feel that way too, and that's part of the film's enduring charm.

Does *your* life feel stuck on repeat? Do you wake up each morning to live out what seems like the same day? Maybe you feel like something in your life is missing. If you feel stuck on a hamster wheel, you are not alone.

I want you to stop just ***getting by***. It's time for you to ***thrive***.

Creativity is the missing ingredient for many of us. Too many years spent grinding away at jobs we hate dull our senses. Have you lost your sense of curiosity? I did, for a long time. In this book, I describe how to connect with your creativity and create space in your life to engage in the activities that bring you energy and joy.

You can change your life with the approach I lay out in this book. Stop living Groundhog Day and choose a creative life where you thrive.

Why are we unhappy?

Many of us work jobs we don't like. Less than half of U.S. workers said they felt satisfied with their jobs overall, according to a 2016 report by the Conference Board. 2016 Gallup figures are worse; they found that only 32% of U.S. employees are engaged with work, and only 13% worldwide.

Consider that we spend 10,500 days at work (assuming five days a week, 50 weeks a year between the ages of 23 and 65). Said differently, we work 36% of the total days that we're alive on this planet (should we live to be 80).

We spend a huge chunk of our lifetime at work, *yet half of us hate our jobs*. No wonder many of us feel stuck on repeat, living each day without much thought.

That's the situation I found myself in a few years ago. I was unhappy. We all have bad days—that's a fact of life—but it was more than that. I was deeply uncomfortable with my situation and the path down which my life was heading. It wasn't about regret. Something important was missing.

Despite feeling unsettled, there was much to be grateful for: good health, loving family, my husband, friends, and living in a peaceful time. I had built a good career, but I wasn't happy with my job anymore. Something was missing.

I lived for the weekends. Sunday nights were the worst because it meant going to work the next day. I became a bucket of angst thinking about the coming work-week and all my obligations.

Then, a close family member died unexpectedly, and I saw friends getting cancer at younger ages. I realized the stuff I'd been told all my life—"Work hard, save all you can so you can afford the big house and retire comfortably"—was not guaranteed to come true for everyone.

I started wondering what would give my life more meaning.

My WWII-generation grandparents worked hard and scrimped most of their lives, only to sit in front of the television day after day in their elder years. After retirement, when they could have traveled, they no longer desired to, or even had the energy for trips.

5

That's not how I wanted my life to be.

I was lucky to have supportive, career-minded friends. Many were passionate about their careers and loved their jobs. But many were like me—showing up at a job they didn't enjoy. I was nearly vegetative on weekends after a long week spent at a nine-to-five job and hours of unpaid overtime.

"There must be more than this to life," I said to myself.

What gives your life meaning? Are you getting by, or are you thriving?

The Myth of Someday

Conventional wisdom in industrialized countries says we must spend the majority of our lives working, buy houses with 30-year mortgages, and save an enormous amount of money for retirement.

Like me, you probably bought into that thinking and spent, or plan to spend, most of your life working toward your eventual retirement.

Now, I agree there's an advantage to putting aside income for your future. Not planning for your future is reckless. However, we are led to believe that we *need* a checklist of material things to live a happy, good life. We need that large house, the new car every two years, and all the stuff that drives our consumer economies. And so we're conditioned to choose a *Groundhog Day* lifestyle where we work hard at a job we don't enjoy to maintain the lifestyle we are told to have.

Work hard, save for later. Put in your time. Pay

your dues. *Someday* is coming.

The myth of someday is putting off pleasure, meaning, and experience because that's what we have been taught. Maybe you were raised to think work is a four-letter word and it's not supposed to be fun. But think again! Does life need to be that way?

Why not discover what makes you happy now? Why not reconnect with the activities that drive your passion and energy so you can move toward a life where you spend time in your happy place?

The myth of someday is when you say, "I'll do x, y, z one of these days…." Perhaps you think you don't deserve to pursue creativity now—that you need to wait. That's what others around you do, right?

You know you've bought into the myth of some-day when you say:

- "We'll go on that dream vacation when we re-tire."
- "If I just put in the extra hours for the next quarter (or for this project, or fill-in-the-blank), I'll be able to take a break after that."
- "I'll write a book someday."
- "I'll be able to spend more time with my family after this year."
- "Maybe I'll consult or start a business after I re-tire."
- "Maybe I'll take that cooking course one of these days."

When you say these kinds of statements, you are living too much for someday and not enough in the now.

Can Creativity Make Us Happier?

Research suggests creative people are happier than everyone else. Why are so few people talking about the impact of creativity on success and happiness?

Disregard the mental image of the starving, depressed artist toiling away in a studio. Anyone can be creative. That's right—you and I can be creative when we open our minds to new situations and exercise the parts of our brains responsible for creativity.

What does the research say?

Forget what you were told about right brain versus left brain. Cognitive neuroscientists have found that the creative process is more complicated than previously thought. Both conscious and unconscious processing takes place. Creativity does not involve a single region or side of the brain.

Consider the following studies on creativity and well-being:

-Researchers at the University of North Carolina at Greensboro randomly sampled the feelings and actions of 79 students over one week using cell phone surveys. People reported doing something creative 20% of the time, and **those who generally reported feeling happy and active were more likely to be doing something creative at the time**. Those who scored higher in openness to experience were much more likely to spend time on creative activities than others.

-Adobe conducted a 2016 survey of 5,000 adults in five countries comparing creativity with personal and professional success. People who self-identified as creative were more likely to identify themselves as innovative, confident, and problem solvers, **and reported being happier** (by 15 percentage points).

In the same study, U.S. creators earned 17% more than non-creators.

-A study divided groups of people into one group that made art and one that evaluated art at a museum. Those who made art scored higher in psychological resilience. Functional magnetic resonance imaging showed that the changes were correlated with differences in connections between different brain regions in the artwork group.

The brain actually *changed* and people became more resilient to stress when being creative and making art.

How often do you engage in creativity? Could this be a missing ingredient in your life?

Decide to Take Action

So, what do we do after realizing our lives are stuck on repeat? How can we possibly step off the hamster wheel and inject more creativity into our lives?

The solution is simple.

I'm hoping you picked up this book and read this far because you're tired, finally, of living Groundhog's Day. It is up to each of us as individuals. You must decide that you want to make a change. Nobody else can convince you.

Once you decide to act, you choose to thrive. No more getting by and living for the weekends. This book can help you start out on your journey to make lasting change and live a more creative life.

Small actions lead to big change.

Don't worry. You don't need to make a drastic change and quit your job tomorrow. This is a journey of lasting change, not rash impulse decisions. Spending a few focused minutes every day on the creative side of your life will lead to big change.

In Part One of this book, I describe how to **discover your creativity**. Often, we've become so immersed in the daily grind that we forget the activities that bring us alive.

Part Two is about how to **create the space in your life to thrive**. I describe how small daily changes can get us to rethink how we live our lives and start to rewire our brains.

Then, in Part Three, I explain how to go about **making lasting change in your life**. I provide tips on changing your mindset, creating habits, and how to avoid getting derailed.

Finally, the last section of the book is made up of three **case studies** of people like you and me who have changed their lives. They found space to create and even build income around their passions.

Create space, not obstacles.

This book is about creating space in our lives. We live in a busy world and are bombarded with more information than previous generations. The film *The Human Face of Big Data* revealed we are exposed to as much information in a day as our 15th century ancestors were exposed to in a lifetime.

It's easy to get distracted and derail ourselves from being happy. We see snippets of other lives through social media and on the news. We usually see two extremes—either the great moments (e.g., friends on vacation) or the worst (grief or negative news and world events).

Creating space around you to lead a creative life where you thrive takes energy. For many of us, that means that we need to establish new boundaries. It doesn't mean turning your back on friends and families or running away from a situation.

Creating positive change means **turning down the noise**—minimizing the negative things that can derail us. For example, changing your daily habits to focus on a single passion that excites you, or abstaining from social media until the afternoon. Those are examples of how you can create space in your life to find more meaning and purpose.

And yet, even when we know that we should make a change, we put up roadblocks against ourselves. I did this for years. I was *that* person—showing up at parties complaining about my job to anyone who would listen.

Here are the **self-created obstacles** that I've said and heard from others:

I'm too old. It's too late for me to start something or pursue a new passion.

False. It's never too late to make changes in your

life. A Chinese proverb says, "The best time to plant a tree was 20 years ago. The second best time is now."

Consider the following list of artists who didn't start until later in life:

- Writer Charles Bukowski finally quit his day job after his first novel was published at age 51.

- Laura Ingalls Wilder began writing at age 44 and published *Little House in the Big Woods* at age 64.

- Author Raymond Chandler lost his job at an oil company when was 44 and decided to become a detective fiction writer.

- Toni Morrison published her first novel at age 40 and was a single mom.

- Morgan Freeman was an off-Broadway actor most of his life, and it wasn't until age 52 that he gained fame for his role in the film *Glory*.

- Millard Kaufman wrote his first novel at age 90.

I'm not creative. I'm no good at anything.

We are all creative and offer unique perspectives. If you can't think of anything you are good at, make a list of activities you enjoyed when you were a child. What were your favorite subjects? What games did you enjoy playing?

You may not feel as though you're good at art because you haven't had any training. Remember, we all start somewhere. The great artists didn't start painting from scratch; they went to school and received years of training.

You also don't need to be perfect when pursuing creativity. Part of the journey toward a creative life is learning along the way. If it were easy, it wouldn't be worth your time.

I won't be able to make enough money if I spend time on a new hobby/pursue a career change. I won't be able to retire.

You don't have to change careers to live a more creative life. Some of you will want to change your careers because you hate your day jobs enough. Trust me, I know the feeling.

Have you written down your retirement plan? What do you want your life to look like in 2 years, 5 years, 20 years? Changing careers doesn't have to be a total trade-in where you start from scratch.

There are many variations of career and lifestyle changes. Think old skill-new skill. What can you bring from your career experience to get you closer to where you want to be?

What worked for me was becoming a freelance consultant using my old skills (project management) to help clients. I moved to hourly, part-time consulting while I built my new business based on new skills (writing and entrepreneurship).

Indie author Joanna Penn, moved from working five days to four as a consultant to enable her to have a full extra working day to build her side business. Eventually, the side income grew to the point where she felt comfortable leaving her day job. She went from crying at her office desk to now earning a multi-six-figure income and expanding her business.

I'm not good enough. I'll fail.

Negative self-talk is possibly the biggest obstacle we face. Making a significant change is tough. Choosing to live a life where you thrive is scary because there's change involved.

But if you're unhappy as I was, if you spend a disproportionate amount of your time thinking about how unhappy you are, then you owe it to yourself to try.

The truth is that you may fail. There are no guarantees. I fail often, but I keep trying until I make it work. That's the attitude—the mindset—we must adopt to be successful.

I don't know how to change.

Change can be scary. We all want to stick within our comfort zones, but significant personal growth comes when we dare to challenge ourselves. In this book, I will share the concept of a growth mindset and how you can use it to your advantage as you move toward making a change in your life.

My friend/family/spouse is not supportive.

Having unsupportive or negative people in our lives can derail us. Often, it's the fear of disapproval that can prevent us from taking steps toward change. In my experience, and in coaching clients, I've seen that the real reaction from family/friends is not as bad as expected.

If a family member rejects your idea or writes it off as stupid or meaningless, that hurts. Often, the person belittling a new idea is doing so from a place of fear. They are likely unhappy. I provide strategies for dealing with negative people in Part Three of this book.

I hope sharing my journey and the successes of others will help you. I urge you to create the space for change and lead a life where you thrive.

Start Something Great

To understand how to become more creative, we need to step back first. We need to take an inventory of our lives and know what got us on the hamster wheel in the first place.

It's not enough to resolve to be happy and say, "I am creative today." Sheer willpower often doesn't work. Just think of how long our New Year's resolutions last.

We must understand the **root cause** of our discontent before we can make lasting change in our lives. Then, we can look at starting something great.

Ask yourself these questions about your life today:

- What activities bring you joy?
- What activities do you dread or find annoying?

• What is your occupation and how do you feel about it?

• When did you first start feeling unhappy? Can you attach a date or an event? If not, that's okay. Sometimes a cause is not readily found.

Often, by asking ourselves a few questions, a cause may jump out at us. For example, someone who relocated to a new city for a job and is unhappy has an apparent root cause.

For many of us, however, the cause is not readily discernible. And that's normal. I couldn't find a cause right away for the discontent that I realized I had in 2013 and 2014.

Ask yourself questions about how you want your life to look in the future:

- If money were no object, how would you spend your days? (That is, after you take all your friends and me on a round-the-world-trip, of course). Practically speaking, what would you do with your time?

- What do you like to do on weekends and vacations?
- What activities would you enjoy doing more? Again, consider your choices regardless of time and money.
- What do you consider to be your dream job? Why?
- What person would you most like your life to resemble? Why?

I answered these questions as best I could. They were difficult to imagine because I had a narrow world view. It was hard to imagine that life could be different.

Eventually, I hit on something. I'm an avid reader and love traveling, exploring, and learning new things. Early in my career, I had enjoyed my work. I was fortunate to travel to new countries and experience people and cultures. I was always learning new things. Years later, my company had years of shrink-age and cost cutting. My company was no longer growing, and neither was I.

New projects where I would learn new skills be-came projects to outsource jobs to cheaper locations or cut costs and benefits. I seemed stuck in an endless loop of conference calls and unproductive meetings. When I tried to introduce changes that would make our work easier, nobody had time to listen.

It dawned on me what was missing. There were three key ingredients that I needed to enjoy my job and my life:

1) **Growth** - All of us should feel that our careers are growing in some way. When those around you emphasize cutting and outsourcing, your company stops investing in you—in your learning and career development.

When a company stops investing in employee training or doesn't discuss your job growth, that's a red flag. You might need to seek employment else-where.

2) **Creativity** - I consider myself a creative person. I like to think high-level strategy as well as get into the weeds. Do you enjoy finding new solutions to do things better? Do you gravitate toward art, movies, books, music? If so, you may be missing the key ingredient of creativity in your work or life.

3) **Variety** - Lastly, I realized that I thrived in an environment where multiple projects were going on. At my old company, there was little variety in my scope of responsibilities. Had there been other projects I could have volunteered for, I would have, but there were no such opportunities.

What are your ingredients to have a happy work and home life? Can you pinpoint the two to three most important elements that you need to thrive? If the answer is no, don't worry. Trust in the process of emergence as you read this book and think about your situation.

In the next section, I explain how to reboot our brains to get us thinking differently about the world.

27

Reboot Your Brain

When I talk about rebooting our brains, I'm referring to changing the way we think about the world and our place in it. We are the products of our genetics and the environments in which we grew up. Our thinking is shaped over time by our experiences. Throw emotion into the mix, and we have a soup of forces swirling around on any given day, driving our happiness.

Researchers have proposed a set-point theory of happiness that maintains that our level of subjective well-being is determined by a combination of heredity and personality traits. Our set-point remains relatively constant throughout our lives, and often returns to a baseline level after positive and negative life events.

This theory bothers me because I don't want to be subject to my biology and environment. I like to think that you and I can change our set-point levels of happiness.

A few years ago, I discovered the work of Stanford psychologist Dr. Carol Dweck. She wrote a book called *Mindset: The New Psychology of Success*. She asserts that mindset plays a significant role in our well-being.

People can be placed on a mindset continuum based on their views of where ability is acquired.

Those with a **fixed mindset** believe that intelligence/talent/ability is innate—you're born with it. Being smart or a talented athlete is fixed and unchangeable. You either have it, or you don't. Think of Michael Jordan—seems like he was born to play basketball, right? And Einstein must have been born a genius.

Then, there are those with a **growth mindset**. These are people who view talent and ability as the result of hard work and effort. Growth mindset people are all about learning, and are willing to put in the time to develop their skills. They realize Jordan and

Einstein didn't pop out of the womb playing basketball and spouting theories about relativity, respectively. They worked hard for many years to achieve success.

Growth mindset people are not afraid of failure. Instead, they ask what they can learn from their failures, and they try again.

Why is a growth mindset so necessary?

Understanding the two mindsets is important because we face challenges throughout our lives. Because every situation is different, we may have a growth mindset toward certain topics, but then we exhibit fixed mindset traits in other areas of life.

What's fascinating about Dweck's research is that you can **change** your mindset. She writes about how she and a group of researchers went to public schools and taught a group of children about the growth mindset.

They told students:

"Many people think of the brain as a mystery. They don't know much about intelligence and how it works. When they do think about what intelligence is, many people believe that a person is born either smart, average, or dumb—and stays that way for life. But new research shows that the brain is more like a muscle—it changes and gets stronger when you use it. And scientists have been able to show just how the brain grows and gets stronger when you learn."

The researchers went on to explain to the kids that the brain forms tiny connections—neurons—that multiply and get stronger when they think and study. The kids learned that the more they challenge their brains, the more their brain cells grow.

Reactions from the children were positive, and in some cases surprising. Dweck writes about one disengaged boy who, upon hearing the explanation, said with tears in his eyes, "You mean I don't have to be dumb?"

The notion of growth mindset versus fixed was a

real eye-opener for me. Maybe it's new to you, too. Dweck writes about how one can apply the growth mindset to challenges in business, relationships, parenting, and athletics.

I advocate that you can apply the growth mindset to problems of feeling unhappy, too. However you're stuck—whether it's a bad job, a toxic relationship, or a rough time in your life—adopting a growth mindset can help.

There have been numerous times when I adopted a fixed mindset, especially early in my career, in past relationships, and more recently when I challenged myself to pursue writing—an ability that I always thought was an innate talent.

As I wrote and inevitably made mistakes, I thought I wasn't good at writing. My fixed mindset thinking made me want to give up. But now, through understanding the growth mindset theory, I realize that it's up to me to challenge myself every day and learn. Success comes through persistence and putting in the time.

How can you benefit from a growth mindset?

How can apply the growth mindset to change your thinking? Here are a few tips from Dweck's book:

Think about the **legacy** you want to leave behind. There's a wonderful quote from the book: "When you're lying on your death bed, one of the cool things to say is, 'I really explored myself.' If you only go through life doing stuff that's easy, shame on you."

Is there something you want badly in life, but are perhaps afraid to try? It took me until age 39 to finally write a book. Over the years, I often thought about getting started, but procrastinated because I didn't realize that I could learn the skills to succeed. Don't let more time pass before you follow your dreams.

Consider how you react to setbacks.

People with fixed mindset have just as much confidence as people with growth mindsets—before anything happens, that is. Dweck points out a study in which employees were taking a computer training course. Half the employees were put into a group and given growth mindset advice: that they could develop their computer skills through practice. The other half, the fixed mindset group, were told that their success was dependent on how much ability they possessed.

The two teams started off with the same confidence in their computer skills, but their results were quite different. The growth mindset students gained considerable confidence in their skills as they learned, despite making many mistakes along the way. The fixed mindset group, however, actually lost confidence in their computer skills as they learned.

Understand that one event does not define your

intelligence or personality. We inevitably go through life feeling as if we're being measured. Whether it's a test score, a job interview, or getting fired or laid off, consider these situations from a growth mindset. Look honestly at your role and avoid thinking about it as a rejection. Instead, ask, "What did I (or what can I) learn from that experience? How can I use this for growth?"

Like your brain, the growth mindset is similar to a muscle. The more you practice growth mindset, the easier it becomes to carry that thinking with you to apply in challenging situations.

I offer up the concept of growth mindset because I believe it is life changing. Growth minded thinking has helped me rewire my brain to focus more on learning. Things that seemed like tough challenges are not insurmountable. You just need to break down the work and embrace it as a learning opportunity.

We need constant reminders to learn to adopt a growth mindset. After all, our brains need a lot of help to rewire. Write the following statements and post them on your wall as a reminder:

   -I learn every day.

   -I embrace challenges and seek to learn.

   -When I fail, I learn a valuable lesson.

   -I try my hardest.

   -If you succeed, I'm inspired and happy for you.

   -My effort and attitude determine my success.

Hello? This Is Life Phoning with Your Wake-Up Call

In 2014, I spent a lot of time obsessing about how unhappy I was at work. My self-worth was tied up in my job title and how much money I earned. I thought that to step away would be a sign of failure.

My first wake-up call came when I was suddenly laid off in 2015. After years spent working hard, the powers that be at my company decided I was no longer required. Getting laid off is an ego blow, especially for those of us who have wrapped our identities around our careers.

What is your identity? Is it work, family, or some combination?

In my twenties and thirties, work was everything. When I went through a divorce, my job was my refuge. It provided me a means to survive, to make a living and buy my first apartment on my own. After I moved to a new city, met new people, and moved on, my company continued to be a solid rock in my life.

And yet, the years spent being loyal to my company were not reciprocated. I felt as though a rug was pulled from under me when they eliminated my job without warning.

So, how do you avoid this happening to you? How do we prevent ourselves from getting trapped into maintaining an identity even though we might not even like it?

My situation may be extreme compared to others, but I think the pattern of working a job we don't like is all too familiar. We're taught by our culture to fit in, to be normal. In school and on TV, we're told to get a normal, steady job. We're told in subtle ways, "Don't push the limits, kid."

Growing up, I heard, "Study hard, get good grades, go to a good school, work hard, climb the ladder, and then retire one day." It's no surprise that my identity was about work.

Does that mean that life starts when we retire? I had never thought about it that way until the job I depended on disappeared. It took a layoff for me to realize I was climbing the corporate ladder with no end. I would never find happiness because there was nothing at the end for me to find.

I thought I had everything figured out: Live a simple life, with work and family being the two most important things. But, I was forced to think again.

Experiencing loss.

There was a second wake-up call that woke me from my single-minded focus on career. My stepfather had stage-four brain cancer.

It was devastating to my family; he lived only three months after the diagnosis. When you watch a loved one die, you realize our limited time on this planet. **What would you do if you learned you had three months to live? How would you spend those**

precious few weeks?

Bronnie Ware is the author of *The Top Five Regrets of the Dying*. She wrote about her experience caring for people approaching the ends of their lives. In order of frequency, the top five regrets were:

1. I wish I'd had the courage to live a life true to myself, not the life others expected of me.

2. I wish I hadn't worked so hard.

3. I wish I'd had the courage to express my feelings.

4. I wish I had stayed in touch with my friends.

5. I wish I'd let myself be happier.

Do any of these regrets resonate with you? I heard similar regrets from my stepfather in his final weeks, and from my grandparents in their later years, too.

The fact that the biggest regrets are about living a true life and working too hard is frightening. We owe it to ourselves to act now and seize the lives we want to lead. It's not the easy thing to do, but it's the right choice.

Discover What You Love

The combination of my stepfather's passing and losing my job made me realize I was not living the life I wanted. I decided to change focus and find meaning through creativity.

How to discover what you love.

First, I began a journey of self-discovery using tools that I'll share with you. I called this a reboot because what I discovered ended up changing my life and caused me to reinvent my life and work.

I had always wanted to write a book…someday. But, something was always holding me back. I thought I didn't have the talent, and had no idea where to start. Writing a book sounded hard, and I was tired most of the time from working a job I hated.

Anyone can use these tools, regardless of their situation. You don't have to go through a layoff or lose someone. In fact, all the better to discover what you love while you still have a job. The steps I recommend can help you better understand yourself. And that leads to taking steps to live a thriving life, and ultimately be happier.

Step 1 - Get organized.

Discovering yourself and awakening your creativity takes energy. Many of us have physical and mental clutter we need to clean out before we can start to thrive. Be sure to take care of business first. If you have pressing family obligations or a major project that needs to be completed, be sure to finish those first before you start this journey.

You may need to do some clearing before you can start this journey of discovery. You're not alone. I had piles of paper—documents, mail, etc.—that I had been ignoring. I set aside a few hours one day and went through it, tossing most of it. If you have something you've been putting off, consider knocking it out. Once you do, you can focus on the next steps.

Step 2 - Make a for-fun list.

Start listing things that interest you, but that you've been putting off because you were too busy. What ideas have been rattling around in your head?

Now, have some fun! Include anything that pops into your head, no matter how silly or far-fetched. Are there things you've dreamed about but never had time to pursue? Include any habits or lifestyle changes you want to make.

Not all these things will happen, but the point is to have fun and dream. Here are some ideas to get you started:

-Write and publish a book.

-Develop a habit of writing every day.

-Lose weight/get toned.

-Learn to cook a few amazing, easy meals that

will impress friends and family.

-Start a blog.

-Learn to knit.

-Volunteer with a local charity.

-Read every day.

-Visit Paris and Italy.

-Laugh more.

-Go to museums and attend art lectures.

-Go on a meditation retreat.

-Become sought after as an expert in your field.

-Travel to the Pacific Northwest.

-Travel to Japan.

-Start a podcast.

-Swim with whale sharks.

-Learn sword fencing.

-Write and direct a movie.

-Start a publishing firm.

-Attend Comic-Con.

-Start painting art.

-Get a massage.

-Learn about minimalism. Reduce clutter in your

house.

Get the idea? Have fun and watch your list grow. This process made me realize all the things I could do if I wanted to focus my time less on my job and more on the things that truly interested me.

Keep a notebook with you to jot down ideas. You'll end up adding to your list over time. I keep my list handy to capture new ideas. The list can keep us on track as we grow and develop. The things that interested you 10 years ago may be much different today.

Refer to this list monthly as a sanity check. Once you have this list, you have the power to choose how you live your life. You are on a path to self-realization. Many people don't give this thought. More often, they go from one day to the next and years pass by in a flash.

I don't ever want to be in a position again where I'm not checking things off this list. I always want to tackle my "fun list." Don't you?

Step 3 - Pick one theme and create a mind map.

While it's exciting to think about your long for-fun list, bear with me. When we decide to make lasting change in our lives, we must choose carefully and **focus on one thing at a time.**

A quote from Bill Gates has stuck with me: "Most people overestimate what they can do in one year and underestimate what they can do in ten years." When I started my reboot, I got swept up in excitement and started thinking I would enroll in a class and volunteer and plan a trip and write a book all at the same time.

But you can't tackle everything at once, unfortunately. We must be selective and start off by making one change at a time. Try to choose one thing from your list.

Did you notice any themes emerging when you made your list? For me, the topic of writing appeared. I had always wanted to write a book, and establishing a writing habit and starting a blog were new things that interested me more than anything else on the list.

Hopefully, a theme emerges for you too.

Have you encountered the technique of mind mapping before? Elementary schools sometimes use it to help kids plan essays. But even as an adult, it's the best tool I've found for releasing creativity and coaxing your brain into pumping out ideas. I had success with the approach when planning large projects. It's a tool I go back to again and again because it works so well.

The first thing you do is write down a central theme or idea in the middle of a page. Next, write down related ideas, so they form branches off your central theme. Get these on paper in any order they come into your head. No editing—the idea is to get all your thoughts down and let your creativity flow. As you keep writing down ideas, you'll even develop sub-branches. Keep brainstorming and capturing your thoughts on one page.

The point of this is to take your theme and mind map your ideas around how to pursue it. Here are several topics to consider.

-Making a career change

-Starting your own business

-Planning an overseas adventure

-Volunteering

-Starting your retirement

-Taking a sabbatical

-Learning to teach yoga

Notice these themes start with action-oriented verbs. You are planning, starting, or making something. Life is no longer happening *to* you, because you are a growth-minded person. You are a doer.

My theme was writing a book, so I included mind map branches such as signing up for an online class, writing every day for 30 minutes, picking a topic, and learning how to self-publish on Amazon.

Think of your mind map as your how-to roadmap. What do you need to learn to get started?

What can help you—classes, teachers, books? What is step one, two, and three? Turn a vague idea into actionable steps.

Another example would be starting a new business to provide software consulting services. First, what does that mean? What services would you provide? List those as separate bubbles (e.g., mobile app development, website development, etc.). How will you deliver those services? Will you make Facebook apps, utilize iTunes, or use another avenue? What do you need to learn first? Do you need to brush up on marketing?

Hang onto your finished mind map, and refer to it as you read this book. It's meant to be a foundational tool. My mind map went through several iterations.

Have fun. Dare to dream big—don't place limits on what you want to accomplish. Play music while you're dreaming up new ideas.

Choosing a theme and making your mind map is important, and a foundation to the rest of this book. I recommend you take a few hours to make your list and create your mind map before you continue reading. However, I realize that many of us like to read a book first and come back to exercises later.

Up next: How to start experimenting and introducing change into your life.

Experiment

You should feel good about starting down the path of self-discovery. How do you feel after having completed your mind map? Are you excited? I hope so, because now is when you start to experiment with making small changes in your life.

Feel good about this process. Don't be ashamed of wanting to understand yourself better. I believe our culture has brainwashed us into thinking about self-discovery as New-Age nonsense. We're conditioned to think, "Good things come to those who wait."

I think that's ridiculous. Whatever age you are, and regardless of your situation, you deserve to take time out to focus on yourself. Follow your passions because life goes by faster than we think.

Is there such a thing as a *calling*?

I was always one of those people who thought a calling wasn't real. That was fixed mindset me talking. How could I ever find a calling when I didn't ever stretch myself? Of course, I didn't know what my passions were when all I did was work.

But, after I undertook this process of self-discovery, I could pinpoint my unique skills and talents. I began to understand myself better, and realized I do have a calling. I uncovered the interests that fuel me. Had I not set aside time following my layoff, I would have missed out.

Maybe you don't have a single calling yet. But I bet you have skills that, when combined with your greatest interests, will give you a clear sense of purpose that is unique. For me, there was something important missing from my old job. I was using my career expertise in project management, but I had lost the essential ingredient of creativity. The people I've met who are happiest with their careers are those who

53

have discovered what really drives them—what energizes them.

How to achieve balance: Experiment.

By now, you may be thinking, "What's next?" You have evaluated your life and thought about what's important and what might be missing.

Next, we use experimentation to reconnect with creativity. Your mind map comes into play here. Whether your idea is to write a book, learn the guitar, or take up trout fishing, you can start to carve out time in your day to focus on that pursuit.

"But, I'm too busy," you're saying. Don't worry; you don't need to carve out a ton of time. One hour per day is ideal, but 30 minutes will do. Commit to spending that time dedicated to and entirely focused on your creative idea.

Maybe you're learning a new skill for the first time. If so, you might spend 30 minutes a day reading books on your topic, or listening to audio or podcasts during your commute. The number of podcasts on virtually every topic imaginable has exploded.

Or perhaps you have the skill already, but you've neglected it for some time. When you carve out your time, you are practicing your skill, be it writing, painting, knitting, or gardening.

Don't fret about not having the time. I'll give you tips to create more time in the next section. I'm going to be brutally honest now, because I had to ask myself these same questions.

How long have you been saying you can't find the time? How badly do you want it? There's always going to be something that comes up in our lives. Life will get in our way. Unless we fight back to make the time for ourselves, we will always lose the battle to other obligations, emergencies, and other people's agendas.

Allow yourself to focus on self-discovery. Resist the feeling that you are selfish. The better you know yourself, the stronger your inner self can shine. And, you'll make a positive impact on those around you.

Part Two: Create Space in Your Life to Thrive

Find the Place

We live in a noisy world and are bombarded with advertisements and competing demands on our time. Worse, we're told how our lives should be lived by media, ads, and the people around us. Digital marketing experts say that Americans are exposed to as many as 5,000 advertisements each day.

Commercials tell us that we need to buy the latest fashions and get a new car because, well, what we have is old. Don't you want *new*? There's a constant quest for the new and latest thing. There's an immediate gratification to acquiring new things, but how long does that last? The new car smell always goes away, and what remains is a car payment.

I realized years ago that I was happier spending my money on things that provided an *experience*. As a kid, I rearranged the furniture in my room every weekend. I was constantly trying to manage my environment—the small space that was my bedroom and no one else's. I didn't know it at the time, but I had minimalist tendencies.

Dealing with clutter.

Clutter is my enemy. In my home, I'm on a constant lookout for clutter. I donate to Goodwill several times a year, when I fill my car trunk with a few months' worth of things that aren't useful.

I love books, and over time have donated many volumes, and moved to buying more books online through my e-reader. A trick for clothing is to hang everything in your closet with the hook facing backward. After wearing an article, hang it up again and turn it in the opposite direction to see what's being worn. Get rid of those clothes not getting used after a few months.

The reason I try to keep my space clean and clear of clutter is that it makes me feel good. Just like when I was a kid, I want to control my environment because clutter makes me feel messy inside my head.

To have space where I can create means that it needs to be organized and clear.

How does your space make you feel? Are you good at clearing out clutter, or do you struggle? If you have a lot of clutter in your house, it's best to start small. Work on the room where you plan to do your creative work first. Start with 15 minutes a day to remove five things. Start a donation pile. Over time, you'll begin to make a space where you can think and create.

Shopping day.

In my household, minimizing clutter means that we reduce the amount of stuff we buy. My husband and I designate a shopping day once a month where we buy items (usually online) on that day only. We've stopped impulse shopping. Throughout the month, I keep a wish list that I save until shopping day. By then, I can't always recall why we needed some of the items.

One in, two out rule.

Another household rule that works for us is to throw two things out for every new item that we bring into the house. This practice isn't always easy to stick to, but we try our best. You can see how, over time, this would help to cut down on clutter.

Finding a physical spot to create.

As you start to experiment and slowly change your life to focus on your creativity, you will need a place in which to work. Make it a place where you can't be disturbed. Put a sign on the door if you must.

You want to get into a state of creative flow, and that may mean putting on headphones and shutting out the rest of the world. If you can't find solitude at home, consider finding a cafe or a library that offers a refuge in which to create.

Sometimes changing your environment helps stir your creative juices. An idea I picked up from author Joanna Penn is cafe-hopping. I'll go to one cafe with my laptop and write for an hour, then go to a second cafe, and possibly a third. That's time to have about three coffees and rack up about 3,000 words.

Clearing digital clutter.

I addressed physical clutter, but what about clutter in your digital life? If you're like me, you have a computer desktop full of icons and files. I receive too many emails, and I create many files throughout the course of a day. I try to organize as I go, but I'm not perfect.

You've probably heard the advice to only to check your emails a few times a day. This is called *batching tasks*—doing similar jobs together at one time for efficiency. Compare this to a day where you manage your work based on incoming emails. How did you feel at the end of the day? Did you feel productive, or could your time have been better spent on other activities?

Once or twice a year, I'll declare *email bankruptcy*. When I've left my emails unopened for too long, or I've gotten too many promotions/newsletters I won't have time to read, I'll archive all the mail, and if I ever need something, I can search to find it.

When I started clearing, I was clinging to articles I would read "someday." They were taking up mental space. So, I deleted them. Consider unsubscribing to most newsletters, only keeping those that will add value to your creativity.

How many items are you hanging onto for someday?

Get away from the usual.

Perhaps, to connect with your creativity, you need to get away from your normal environment. Maybe home is not conducive to creating. Have you ever tried going to a cafe with your laptop? Or, consider bringing a sketchpad or notebook and see where your thoughts take you.

Where else can you find creative refuge if your home doesn't provide it? Can you visit the library or another public space such as a museum? When I worked across the street from the Art Institute of Chicago, I bought an annual pass so I could go there on lunch breaks and experience the art to take a mini-vacation from my boring day job.

Maybe your home is still the best place for you to create. How can you shake things up? Can you try using a different room in the house? How much do you use that guest bedroom? Why not turn it into a studio and make guests sleep on the living room couch? Ultimately, it's up to you to find the best spot to create. I recommend trying new things out to find what works best for you.

Wherever you decide to pursue your creativity, it should feel comfortable and be easy for you to get to when you need it.

Create the Time

We all struggle with finding time. In fact, the number one complaint I hear from people I coach is that they can't find the time to write more or market their books or do other things that are equally important.

In this section, I offer ideas of how you can create more time in your life by making choices with your day. These strategies have helped me, and I hope you find my tips useful.

Reduce time spent on social media.

Our social networks have expanded. Consider now that you can locate friends from grade school, high school, and college on social media sites such as Facebook and LinkedIn. Before the rise of social media, we would have lost touch with these acquaintances or maybe run into them years later at a reunion event.

I'm not saying social media is bad. Far from it. Having the ability to connect with others around the world is a marvel. It provides us the potential for creative freedom. We don't necessarily need to put on a suit and tie and head to a physical office to make a living. Many people are making a living online. In 2015, there were an estimated 24 million entrepreneurs in the United States, which represented 14% of the working-age population.

Social media adds to our lives, but there is a dark side. It makes for a noisy world. Along with family, work, traditional media such as TV, and news, social media competes for our attention, often to the detriment of relationships with others. Have you ever stopped to look around at a restaurant to see how many people are on their phones even though they are dining in the company of others?

For adults, we can feel stressed or anxious when we see the "highlight reels" of others on Facebook and Instagram. I speak from personal experience when I say that it can seem like our lives aren't measuring up when we constantly see others out enjoying themselves, traveling and on vacation. We don't hear as much about the bad day they had, or that their car broke down.

Look at your social media habits. Have you found yourself anxious when looking at social media? On a scale of 1 to 10, how much of your time each day goes toward social media? Is it one hour or a few hours? Multiply that by seven days to see how much time you spend in a week. Then multiply that by 52 to see how much time you spend per year.

I'm not saying time on social media is all bad. It's easy to snap a quick picture on your phone and send it out to the world. It's a way to keep in touch with distant friends and loved ones. For some grandparents, it gives them a glimpse into the daily lives of their grandchildren.

Instead, I'm asking you to be honest with yourself about your social media habits. Does your time on social media add to your life and happiness? Or, could you eliminate some of the time you spend on social media and use it for something else in your life?

This is what I mean by creating the space in your life to thrive. If you're spending three hours a day on social media, how about cutting that by one hour? That adds up to a savings of 364 hours a year (or nine 40-hour work weeks) that you could put toward cultivating a new passion.

Make the first hour of your day matter.

Creating a morning routine has been the biggest game-changer for many clients and me. The approach is simple: Dedicate the first hour after you get up to your most important thing. For me, it's writing. I get up and grab a coffee and sit down to write. I set a timer, so I know I write a full hour.

You can spend that time doing anything you like—just make sure it's something that's important to you. If you're working on a side business, use the first hour to learn how to land more clients, or use the time to network online.

My husband changed his day-job shift to accommodate a morning routine. Before, he got up early and worked 7:30 am to 4:30 pm. He was too tired in the evenings to spend time on growing his side business. Then, he changed his shift to start work at 9:30, and instead uses the early morning time for his projects.

What's most powerful about a morning routine is that we're able to tackle our most important activities with fresh, rested brains. That's when we're the most efficient. When we try the reverse—to work on important things after a long day—we're mentally exhausted from making so many decisions throughout the day. A study that compared morning and evening brains scans found that mornings showed more neural connections in the brain—a key element to the creative process.

If science tells us that we're most creative in the

morning, after a night of sleep, then what are you doing with that important first part of your day?

How are you using your weekends?

For most of us, the weekends are for rest, spending time with family, and going to church if you're religious. But, could you use that time differently? Could you carve out a part of Saturday and Sunday as your own?

Many clients with families will rise early on weekends and get important work out of the way first thing so they can spend the rest of the day attending to family matters.

I used to go out and spend lots of money on restaurants and events on Friday and Saturday nights. I still go out a few times a month, but much less than in younger years. It's just not as important as it once was.

With that lifestyle, I would stay out late and then sleep in the next mornings, sometimes not rising until

11:00 am or noon. Nowadays, I usually stick to the same early wake-up schedule for weekends because it's important for me to use the time to write and work on growing my business.

What can you give up?

What can you give up for an extra hour of consistent time every day spent pursuing what you love? Can you:

- Get up one hour earlier?
- Give up watching TV at night?
- Hire a cleaning service?
- Have your groceries delivered?
- Delegate dinner preparation to someone else in your family?
- Have lunch alone every day and spend time on your new pursuit?

My husband and I got rid of cable and cut down

our TV viewing time. We still stream an hour or two of our favorite shows each night, but losing the commercials has been a time saver.

Other time-saving techniques:

• Ladies, consider wearing minimal makeup and letting your hair air dry.

• Lay out clothes the night before so you're not stuck deciding what to wear.

• Hire a cleaning service once every two weeks.

• Every other week, have a service deliver groceries to save 1.5 hours.

• Can you change your commute? If you go in a bit later, will you miss the rush hour traffic?

Some of these ideas may seem extravagant, but hiring people to clean, get groceries, or walk your dog pays off when you consider the time you can put toward creating and going after creative activities that make you happy.

Change your relationship with your day job.

Are you in a situation where you struggle to find time outside your day job? If so, you may need to take a hard look at whether that's how you want to spend your working life.

Unfortunately, I worked my corporate job on weekends and most evenings to "catch up" because of overload. Family obligations, household chores, and everyday life required the rest of my attention. How often do you find yourself working *extra* because someone else can't do the job or your leadership didn't plan and hire enough staff?

When your life becomes dominated by another person's work, you are doing yourself a disservice. I finally asked myself what I was doing working weekends at this job. I was already putting in 50+ hours a week. Enough was enough. I decided that the job was not a good fit for me if I was too drained to spend any time on what mattered to me most—writing and creativity. Instead, I decided to start my own business and become a freelance project manager. This was a tough decision, but necessary to live the creative life I was seeking.

If you're unhappy in your job, how can you change your situation? Can you work your job at the minimum hours per week? Are there changes you can make to spend more time on your creativity? Does a company bonus really matter if it requires more time and commitment from you?

A 2010 Princeton study showed there's a correlation between the level of happiness and income up until you reach a $75K salary, but after that, there's no significant change in happiness the more you earn. Adjusted for cost of living data, the number increased to $83K in 2015. Other factors play into this, such as the size of household and personal happiness needs, but the notion that we must earn high salaries to become happier does not prove out.

Author Joanna Penn went from working five days to four days a week to build her income to a point where she could quit her day job entirely. My husband changed his work shift, so he could have two hours during mornings to work on personal projects. These decisions can be tough but worth it when you consider that you're creating space in your life to thrive.

Find Energy

After you find the right place and create time to pursue new creative avenues, you need to work on finding energy. This means learning to take care of yourself.

Maybe you're saying, "But I have my kids, family, mother, etc. And they take up my time." I know it can be tough to make room in your life to go after your creativity, but you must try your best.

Is there something—anything—you could give up? Or, something you could change in your routine? Can another family member pick up your kids from school once or twice a week so you can have some alone time?

Or, maybe you bring your kids or your significant other along with you on this creative journey. Maybe the kids could play in the park while you write or sketch. Open your heart and mind to new possibilities. You might be surprised what happens when you vary your routine.

Sleep.

We've all heard the maxim that we need eight hours of sleep each night. It turns out we actually need the amount of sleep that's best for each of us. Not too little and not too much.

Researchers at the Finnish Institute of Occupational Health found that there is a sweet spot for getting the right amount of sleep (about 7.76 hours). They found that people who overslept or underslept had more days absent. I use a sleep tracker (e.g., Fitbit) to track my weekly average. There's a noticeable difference in my quality of life on those days following a bad night's sleep.

How well do you sleep now? Consider how much quality sleep you are getting. Do you think you need more? What can you adjust?

We often blame lack of sleep for issues, but I

went through a phase where I was oversleeping. Using a sleep tracker helped me realize that I felt worse even though I was getting nine-+ hours of sleep. I changed up my lifestyle, exercise, and eating habits to get back on track.

Nutrition.

Michael Pollan, author of *The Omnivore's Dilemma,* said, "Eat food. Not too much. Mostly plants." I try to use that guidance when making food choices.

Our food affects so much that happens in our lives—how we feel throughout the day, our moods, and our overall health and well-being.

If weight or eating is a major issue for you, I urge you to consult your doctor. There are many options available to help people, including nutrition programs, counseling, etc.

I ate tons of fast food and went through a frozen

food phase when I was single where I ate a diet almost entirely made up of Lean Cuisine meals. I justified it to myself, saying that I was busy and constantly on the go. I later paid for it when I gained weight I couldn't lose.

It can be tough to make a shift toward healthier food, but we owe it to ourselves to treat our bodies well. After all, we need healthy bodies because our brains have a lot of creative thinking to churn through.

Exercise.

We can't talk about food and sleep without mentioning exercise. Maybe you're thinking, "Yeah, I've heard this all before." But, do you have a regular exercise routine that you follow?

We want our creative selves to shine, and for that to happen, we need happy, healthy brains. That's why it's important we take care of our bodies with exercise.

Years ago, I used to think that exercise meant joining a gym and running or doing cardio for hours upon hours. I hate running; it's boring to me. If you enjoy it, that's terrific. I have friends who can't get enough of running.

But, that wasn't me. I felt weird at the gym. I wasn't like all of the others who seemed happy to work out on elliptical machines for two hours. I wanted to be in and out quickly.

Later, I was pleased to find that I wasn't alone. I learned about short-duration, high-intensity workouts that dramatically increased my muscle tone and helped me lose weight. A side effect was having additional energy and clarity of thought.

Despite all the research studies that point to the positive impact of daily activity, why don't many of us have exercise routines? My guess is that it's not necessarily a lack of time. In the time I spent today on social media, I could have gotten in a 20-minute workout. Instead, the cause is that we don't have a routine in place that encourages exercise and makes it easy for us.

When it comes to heading to the gym or going out for a run, it's easy to skip and make an excuse. When you add something such as an accountability partner or a reward/punishment, you'll see better results.

Or, better yet, build exercise into your everyday routine. Since I like to maximize my time, I use a treadmill desk. I'll often use this while I'm working to try to get in 10,000 steps a day, or as many as I can manage. Otherwise, my day can be sedentary since I spend a lot of time at my computer.

How can you build activity into your daily life? Start small. Even walks outside, a short run, or 15 minutes of yoga can boost your energy. You don't need to spend money on a gym or expensive equipment. I purchased a small, fold-up stationary bike from Amazon, and enjoy reading while biking a few times a week.

Expose yourself to natural light.

Finding natural light is challenging for those of us in northern climates who want to hibernate during the winter. The California Energy Commission conducted a study and found that people who sat near a window performed better, processing tasks 6-12% faster and performing 10-25% better on tests that involved mental function and memory.

I recommend situating your desk near windows if possible. In the winter, I use a sun energy light lamp, which helps relieve the winter blues in those cold months when I don't get outside as much.

If you're lucky enough to live in a warmer climate, be sure to get outside a few times a day to soak up some natural rays. Wherever you live, open those windows and let some light through.

I hope this section is useful to you in some way. I know that we hear about these topics often, but many of us don't step back and look at ourselves hon-

estly to see how we can make lifestyle improve-
ments. To have a happy journey, we must be healthy
in spirit and body.

Part Three: Change Your Life

Beginning to Thrive - The First 30 Days

"What gets measured gets improved." - Peter Drucker

Congratulations for coming this far on your journey toward living a life where you thrive. Let's recap.

First, you picked up this book because, like me, something is missing in your life. In the first section, you asked yourself tough questions and discovered not only what you are missing, but how you can reconnect with your creativity. You pinpointed what you love to do.

Next, you considered how to create space in your life to do what you love. Whether it's writing, painting, or video gaming, you are now armed with ideas to find the place, time, and energy to pursue your passions.

What now? You are excited to get started. In the

first week or so, it can feel like you're walking on air. You wake up early, excited to get started. But, it's not always easy to keep the momentum going. Some things come up that can derail us.

Inevitably, we miss a few days here and there, and that's okay. That's a regular part of our learning process. You see, what you're really doing is building a habit. To fully become a part of our life, habits take time to form.

One of the best ways to adopt a new habit is to track your progress. I love the Peter Drucker quote about measurement. Tracking your results is a key to making effective change. As you begin this journey, find something to measure. Maybe it's word count if you're a writer.

Or perhaps, if you are learning a new skill, you can measure the hours spent taking online courses and reading. If you love playing the violin, measure the hours spent practicing.

It's easy to measure your progress using simple tools. I started out using a spreadsheet. Now, I use a

Google sheet so I can update it online from any-where. Another idea is to take a paper calendar and write in your progress each day. You can give your-self a sticker each day you spend on your creativity.

Over time, your efforts add up. The compound effect is powerful. Consider that writing 1,000 words a day adds up to 365,000 words in a year. Practicing your guitar 90 minutes a day is 548 hours a year, or thirteen 40-hour work weeks. Imagine taking 13 weeks of vacation to work on nothing but your crea-tivity. Sounds like a dream come true, right? It can be your reality if you work on it every day. Do the math about your time; it may surprise you.

The average time spent on social media globally in 2016 was 118 minutes per day. That's 693 hours a year, or seventeen 40-hour weeks. I find this figure staggering. I'd rather spend the extra hour or two of my day having something to show for it. For me, I'll have 365,000 words written, which is the equivalent of six 60,000-word novels.

To sum up: Track your progress. Keep it simple

and take it slow. Your progress daily may feel slow, but consider the compounding effect over time. Don't beat yourself up when you have a bad day. Even spending five minutes on your creativity is better than nothing at all.

Making a Habit: 60 Days In

In his book *The One Thing*, author Gary Keller cites studies that show it takes 66 days to build a habit—not 21, as is commonly touted. A study led by Phillippa Lally looked at habit formation among 96 volunteers over 12 weeks who had to choose a new behavior to start after breakfast each day. The time it took participants to make the new activity an automatic habit ranged from 18 to 254 days. Clearly, there is considerable variation among people when it comes to forming habits.

When it comes to building habits and making lasting change, this means we have a bigger hurdle to face than we thought. How do we set ourselves up for success?

First, I'll offer some tips that have helped me sustain my writing habit over time.

When I started, there were many times I struggled before my writing became routine. Some days I entered a zero because I couldn't find the time or energy to write. But I kept at it, and now getting up to write as the first thing in my day has become natural.

Steps to build a consistent daily creativity practice:

- Track your progress every day.

- Make your new activity the first thing you do every day. Having a morning routine where you get up early and focus first on creativity has worked for me and many others. Look at the number of self-help books on the topic of morning routines if you don't believe me.

- Avoid distractors like email and social media until later. Don't look at emails first thing in your day if you can avoid it. If you must because your job has emergencies that come up, then quickly scan your email and then put it away.

- Start small. Don't try to wake two hours early at first. Start with rising 30 minutes early and see how that goes for a week until you're ready to try one hour.

•Be consistent with the time of day that you create. Our brains like simple cues when forming a habit.

•On weekends, schedule blocks of time and protect it like you would an important appointment. Weekends can be a good time to make up for lost time during the week.

•Once a week, set aside 20 minutes to review your progress. Are there obstacles getting in your way? How will you deal with them in the week ahead? What are your lessons learned? What would you do differently?

•Consider finding an accountability buddy. Is someone else in your life hoping to make a change? Message or call them once a week and report how you're doing.

Remember that nothing is forever. Think of the first two months as an experiment. If you fail on your first try, you can always start over. If you don't like what you're doing as much as you thought, then try something else. Make it your choice.

Adopt the Growth Mindset

"People in a growth mindset don't just seek challenge; they thrive on it." - Carol Dweck

We talked about rebooting your brain in Part One. To make lasting change in our lives, to live a life where we step off the hamster wheel and thrive, we need to change our mindsets.

What got us here isn't working. It's time to make a change, and we must accept that the change is good.

To accept change, we must adopt the growth mindset. We want to move away from the fixed mindset.

Recall that people with a **fixed mindset** believe that intelligence/talent/ability is innate—you're born with it. Being smart or a talented athlete is fixed and unchangeable, whereas growth mindset people view talent and ability as the result of hard work and effort. Growth mindset people are about learning, and are willing to put in the time to develop their skills.

How the fixed mindset harms us.

Those with a fixed mindset believe intelligence is static, and therefore there's a desire to look smart. Here are nine signs that you have a fixed mindset:

1. You avoid challenges.

2. Your confidence is crushed when you go through a setback.

3. You criticize yourself a lot.

4. When things become hard, you get defensive or give up easily.

5. You might be carrying something from your past that you think measured you—test scores, being rejected, being fired from a job.

6. You refrain from starting something new even though you always wanted to do it.

7. When you feel down or depressed, you let

things go.

8.   You feel threatened by the success of others.

9.   You handle negative criticism poorly and ignore it.

Those with a fixed mindset tend to see things as black and white. In our education system, people get fixed with a label of "gifted," and then later struggle when they fail a test. Carol Dweck's research found that telling students they are smart made them eventually feel dumber and act dumber, but claim they were smarter than they were.

Don't worry if you display some of these characteristics. We all have these tendencies some of the time. The good news is you can train your brain to become growth-minded.

How the growth mindset helps us.

When you have a growth mindset, you believe intelligence can be developed, which leads to a desire to learn. Therefore, you:

1. Embrace challenges.

2. Persist in the face of setbacks.

3. See effort as the path to mastery.

4. Learn from criticism.

5. Find lessons and inspiration in the success of others.

Compare the long-term effects of both mindsets. People with fixed mindsets may plateau early and achieve less than their full potential. Examples of fixed mindsets include Lee Iacocca and the leaders of Enron and AOL. The CEOs of these companies ran their businesses into the ground because of their desire to enhance their feelings of self-worth and importance at the expense of their employees.

Growth-minded individuals experiment, learn from their mistakes, and reach ever-higher levels of achievement. Think Oprah Winfrey, Jack Welch, and

Lou Gerstner. These leaders adopted a more nurturing culture that was open to new ideas and learning.

Perhaps these are extreme examples. Most of us will never be and don't desire to be a CEO. But surely you've experienced people who were stuck in a fixed mindset. Maybe you even tried to help them out of it.

How to adopt the growth mindset.

Carol Dweck offers suggestions to become a growth-minded person:

- Set up a daily reminder for yourself about the differences between fixed and growth mindsets. List out the traits above and tape it to your wall or put it in your phone.
- Then, ask yourself, "What are the opportunities for learning and growth today? For me? For the people around me?"
- Next, ask yourself, "When, where, and how will I

embark on my plan?"

- Consider any obstacles that might get in your way. How will you deal with them?

You don't need to make this a complicated plan that you write out. Have a quick dialog with yourself each morning. The important thing is to continue to think about being growth minded.

How to defeat negative self-talk.

One of the most powerful ways to use the concept of growth mindset is to overcome negative self-talk. When I decided to pursue my creativity by writing, I struggled with the inner critic in my head who told me I wasn't good enough. I would tell myself:

I'm not good enough to be a writer. I have no credentials.

I will fail.

People will laugh at me.

There's no way I will ever make any money with my writing.

As I wrote my first book, the self-talk wasn't so bad, but as time went by and I didn't have the immediate success I expected, the criticism became worse. Every day, these thoughts would run through my head.

I became jealous when I saw other aspiring authors have more success. Thinking I'd made a huge mistake, I gave up on writing. Only when I discovered Dweck's book and the growth mindset theory did I change my perspective. I felt as if she had written about me. I had been living in a fixed mindset most of my life.

I defeated my negative self-talk, and so can you. How? Tell yourself you are worth making a change. Realize the creative process is a journey—it will take time, and you will learn as you go. By embracing change and learning from your failures and successes, you will achieve things you didn't think were possible.

Repeat these positive statements to yourself every day. Write down: "I am creative. I am learning, and I am growing." Hang it on your wall where you can see it every day when you get up.

The change in mindset doesn't happen overnight. You need to work at it. Over time, you will see a difference.

Tips for making lasting change.

How do we make lasting change? Visual reminders are a good way to remind yourself about the change you want to make. Consider creating a bulletin board or a Pinterest board where you can see important reminders.

Another idea is to have a daily affirmation. I keep several affirmative phrases in the notes section of my phone. I pull these up first thing each morning and repeat them to myself several times. When we continue repeating these powerful phrases, our brains start to believe the messages we are telling ourselves.

But things don't happen by magic. Just because we make a statement doesn't mean it will magically happen. We must back up our statements with action.

Watch Out for Derailers

Unfortunately, not everyone gets it. It takes serious brain rewiring to lead a life where you thrive. Too many of us have been conditioned to accept what's good enough. Or, we place limits on ourselves because we don't understand what's possible.

To understand how to lead a life where you thrive, you need to know what might derail you.

A thriving life is a journey and a mindset. Every day is not going to be perfect. There will be obstacles that get in your way.

There are three main types of derailers:

1. People
2. Time thieves
3. Energy disrupters

People.

By far, the biggest reason we can get derailed

from choosing to thrive is the people that surround us. We certainly can't choose our family members, and we can't always choose the people we work with either.

In my life, and with clients, I've often seen that most problems in our lives stem from the expectations or actions of the people in our lives.

One of my clients had an entrepreneurial streak. He was a writer, and was slowly building a life where he could thrive—through a side business—while working a demanding day job and supporting his wife and two children.

Unfortunately, his wife wasn't supportive. She didn't, or couldn't, envision his dream of starting his own business. She wanted him to keep his well-paying day job, even though he wasn't happy working it anymore.

Many times, our family members mean well but are acting from a place of fear. Fear of change can influence how we act and the decisions we make.

Change can be scary. That's why I recommend taking small, consistent steps toward moving to a life where you thrive.

In the situation of an unsupportive spouse, consider other tactics. Try showing them evidence of the changes you are making, of how the change will lead to a better life. Maybe that means more time spent with family. Perhaps it's six months of royalty checks from your side business.

It can be challenging to deal with family members who don't have the same mindset as you. My best advice is to persist and gently steer them in the direction of the life you're pursuing.

In my experience, I've dealt with this when my husband didn't understand why I was pursuing being a writer and an entrepreneur. He had once owned his own business, and had a bad experience where he was working insane hours. Out of love, he didn't want that life for me.

When I persisted in creating a vision for what my

life would look like, he started to understand. I wrote one book, then another and another. I built my website and landed my first paying client. That's when the puzzle pieces started coming together. He understood, and during my journey he became incredibly supportive.

Family members can also influence the path we take. Countless people have been steered down career paths by well-meaning parents. Think of the number of doctors or lawyers who may not have naturally gravitated toward those careers, but did so out of family obligation.

Or, the daughter who takes over the family business because that's the way it has been for generations.

Many of my coaching clients are in situations where they took a career path, spent 10+ years doing the work, and now find themselves dissatisfied. They want to start new careers or businesses. Often the new business is unrelated to their jobs; they have discovered a forgotten or neglected passion.

They may be nervous about disappointing their parents or other family members. Often, it's the fear of disapproval that can keep someone in a career for years before they finally make a change.

My clients often discover that the actual reaction from family and friends is not that bad. They are usually surprised when they receive positive responses.

When contemplating a big career change decision, I coach clients to imagine the worst-case scenario. Write it down, in detail. Then consider whether it's that bad after all.

In 99% of cases, the worst-case scenario won't happen. We can live with the outcome. We'll survive.

How do you deal with a negative black hole?

Some of us have people in our lives who have extremely negative outlooks. This is the toughest situation to deal with, especially if we care about those people.

I have dealt with this in my life. First, with a friend that would become openly angry and destructive about events in his life. He had problems, and I tried to help, but it got to the point where I couldn't deal with his angry outbursts anymore. I couldn't take the negative energy, and I made a hard decision to distance myself.

Another situation was a coworker who had a negative outlook on life. If it was a sunny day outside, this person lamented that it would rain tomorrow. Perhaps out of a sense of fear or anxiety, this person looked for the negative in every situation. I'm convinced that he believed that somehow talking about all the things that could go wrong would, somehow ward off adverse events.

As you can imagine, this was an energy drainer, a mood killer, and made it tough to be around this person without feeling stress.

Over the years, I've learned to cope by making positive comments. Often I just keep my mouth shut.

I've tried to change the mindset or bring up the problem, but it is like banging my head against a wall.

We must accept that some people will not change. The best we can do is live our lives to the best of our abilities and serve as examples to others.

One of the biggest changes in my life from just getting by to leading a life where I thrive is finding happiness that wasn't there before. I have a more positive outlook on life. I've learned to handle things that would stress me out in the past. As a result, I have become more organized, have stronger relationships with those I care about, and feel as though I'm living my days with purpose.

Time thieves.

The next category that can derail us relates to how we spend our time. To live thriving lives, we must put in the time to create and pursue our passions.

We must be focused with our time because there is precious little of it.

We must watch out for two time thieves:

Time sucks.

Think of these as the things you choose to spend time on that, while fun at the moment, are distracting you from creating space in your life for what matters.

Video games, television, and social media can be time sucks. They can distract us from creating space to thrive.

I'm not saying that these activities in small doses are wrong. What I recommend is that you track your time for a week or two. Often, we don't realize how much time we're spending checking social media throughout the day. Are you putting in the quality, focused time to create the new life you want to lead?

Ask yourself honestly what you could give up to

reach your goals. Do you really need Candy Crush on your phone? Consider removing social media applications from your computer or phone. Some of us need to disable Internet connectivity entirely to achieve focus.

Time bandits.

Time bandits are tricky. They masquerade as productive time. The biggest culprit is email. In my corporate day job, I made the mistake that so many of us make. I prided myself on being responsive to emails, and ended up managing the time spent at my job by email.

Another time bandit culprit is a long To Do list. I'm a project manager who led global projects impacting up to 60,000 people. When you are building a complex software system, you need an extensive plan with thousands of tasks, but for most of us going about our daily lives, we think we need to accomplish way more than we need to.

In *The One Thing* by Gary Keller, he argues that successful people focus on the one activity that makes them exceptional. They pride themselves on the things they choose NOT to do. Said differently, a writer's one thing is to write, and she needs to focus at least four hours out of the day on writing. Likewise for a tennis pro or a carpenter.

In today's information age, we're all tasked with administration and communications tools such as email. But, these are distractions from our one thing. Consider that when an email comes in, it's a request by someone else. By choosing to spend your time on it, you are choosing to focus on their agenda.

Email is a tool. It should be considered as an accessory to help us communicate and get things done. It should not consume our days.

Other time bandits are housework, chores, and errands. Yes, we need to live our daily lives and buy food for ourselves and our families. We need to ensure our children are healthy and have our attention and support.

My challenge to you: How can you tackle these must-do tasks creatively?

For example, can you delegate household chores to family members and encourage a reward system to make housework more fun? What about outsourcing? Having groceries delivered and house cleaners every two weeks has given me back hours of productive time.

You might be thinking, "But I have small children, and they have sports events every weekend." Again, how can you get creative? Can your spouse cover some of the games and give you a break? Can you bring your laptop with you, or listen to motivational podcasts while you're at the game?

Do nothing time is okay.

I bring up the examples of time thieves to educate, not to preach. These approaches to managing time have worked for my clients and me. I realize everyone has their own situation and responsibilities.

I would never advocate ignoring your family obligations.

And, I don't want you to think that you must be a time efficiency nut. Instead, I challenge you to consider how you're spending your time. Where do you want to be? What do you want to accomplish in one year? In five years? Are you on a path that will get you there?

Always start small. Look at removing one time bandit or making one change at a time. Too much change at once leads to failure.

Time set aside for doing nothing can be the best time we spend. It's time when you can dream. You can consider the progress you've made. Do nothing time is time to reset your body and mind.

Energy disruptors.

Everything in moderation. Sometimes we can go to extremes when it comes to our lifestyle choices. For example, I enjoy drinking wine with dinner, but when I have an evening with friends and the wine flows, I can feel terrible the next day.

A quote I like is "When you drink alcohol, you are borrowing happiness from tomorrow." We can have too much of a good thing. Too much drinking at once, or too many consecutive days in a row, can lead to not feeling well, and that impacts my writing productivity. When I've over-indulged, my energy is drained the next day.

Now, I'm careful and avoid having more than two glasses at a time because I know that my next day won't go well for my writing. So back to the question: What are you willing to give up for the life you want? I don't sacrifice having fun or the quality of my social life. Instead, I make different choices—having water instead of another wine, or going home early. I still have fun, but my priorities have changed, and I want to feel good for the next day. Back when I hated my job, the next day didn't matter. I had nothing to get up for in the mornings.

Is there anything that you might be over-indulging in that could be disrupting your energy? Other disruptors might be overeating, over-exercising, or compulsive shopping. Ask yourself why you go to extremes when it comes to this disruptor. Do you need to give it up entirely, or can you pull back and handle it in small doses? How does overdoing it make you feel? Do you feel the after-effects right away, or some time later (e.g., when your credit card bill comes if you're gambling to fill a gap in your life)? It's possible that focusing your energy on creativity can take the place of the disruptor, but if you can't shake going to extremes, you should consult a counselor.

Putting It All Together

You are creative. You can change your life. Now you have the tools to put everything together and make meaningful, lasting change in your life.

What do you want the rest of your life to look like?

When I first met my husband, he asked me this question. My mouth dropped open. The 31-year-old workaholic me was shocked that a boyfriend would ask this. I was blindly moving forward with my life. I had never thought about such a question. For some reason, it was the exact question I needed to hear at that time in my life. He helped me step back and think about life differently.

I'm a stubborn person, though, and it took me nearly 10 years to make meaningful change in my life. Despite him asking me a life-changing question,

I continued to be a workaholic, and pushed aside my creativity. He still married me—luckily!—and was patient despite my long hours and hearing me complain about work as soon as I arrived home from my ridiculously long commute.

Be patient. Sometimes the change we need most in our lives is painful. Our long-ignored creativity sits in the back of the classroom with its head down. Only when we start asking enough questions and devoting attention every day does creativity find its courage.

What about you? How do you want the rest of your life to look? What do you want others to remember about you? I challenge you to use this book as a guide to taking action.

To recap:

Part One was **discovering what you love**. What are the activities that bring you alive and that exercise your creative muscles? Brainstorm a list and use mind mapping to plan your next steps. Go back and reread the section where I introduced the growth mindset. It's a critical thought process to living a life where you thrive.

Part Two explained how to **create the space in your life to thrive**. There were three key ingredients: 1) finding a simple, clutter-free place to engage your creativity, 2) creating time by giving up other activities that may not be helpful, 3) finding the energy to create through healthy living.

Then, in Part Three, you learned how to **make lasting change in your life**. You are now armed with tips on changing your mindset, creating habits, and how to avoid getting derailed.

How will you continue to move toward a creative, thriving lifestyle? It's easy to pick up a book like this, read it, and think, "Sure, that sounds good." And it's even easier to throw the book aside and never think about it again. I'm guilty of this with many self-help books I read over the years.

I encourage you to create an action plan. To make this easy for you, I've created a companion workbook that you can download from my website. You can print it out and use it as a journal. Go to project-managerwriter.com/thrivebonus now to get it. Start small and dedicate just 15 minutes a day to working on your plan.

Once you've downloaded the workbook, read on to the last section of this book where I share several inspirational stories. These are **case studies** of others who have changed their lives. They found space to create and even build income around their passions. I hope you will find their experiences helpful as you start your creative journey.

Inspiration: Case Studies

Andre: A Passion for Personal Style

"How do you express yourself when everything around you seems to want you to conform? How do you share your personal style with those who may not "get" you? Confidence. Confidence is defined as a feeling of self-assurance arising from one's appreciation of one's own abilities or qualities."

- blackgarmentbag.com

I met Andre when we both worked at the same company, and he joined as a compensation consultant.

Many people don't know what a compensation consultant does. I'll spare the details and just say there are many spreadsheets, and research and analysis are involved. The core of the job is making sure people are getting paid fairly and reasonably per the job market.

Friendly and easy-going, Andre quickly gained a

reputation as being smart, hard-working, and collaborative. We worked together for several years, and he went on to work for other companies, continuing in compensation roles.

When we worked together, I noticed that Andre was good at keeping boundaries. He put in his time at the office and was productive, and he had more balance than other coworkers and me. He didn't linger after work, trying to "catch up" as I did (due to my poor lack of planning and inability to say no).

From a love of fashion to starting his own business.

Years passed, and I met up with Andre again over drinks and group trivia with friends at a downtown Chicago bar. He seemed energetic and happy. He had always been a happy person, but we had also shared our gripes about work in the past. I knew that the energy he was putting out wasn't work-related.

He proudly handed me his business card. He had started his own business—personal styling and fashion consulting. I was thrilled for him. He said he'd started his side business to pursue his love of fashion.

He's since traveled to Milan to shop in the Italian merchandise markets. And, this year, he'll travel to New York and Paris to attend both cities' Fashion Weeks. Andre has an Instagram following of over 600 (and growing). You can find him online at instagram.com/blackgarmentbag.

Here's how Andre created space in his life to pursue his passion.

Finding the place.

Q: Where do you work on your side business?

Andre: For personal styling services, I go to the client's home or meet at a retail shop. For writing my blog and social media interactions, I can do that anywhere. Sometimes, I write on the train or while I'm standing in line at Starbuck's. I can really write and post from anywhere.

Q: How do you get inspired? How do you "fill your creative well?"

Andre: I am inspired by everything from architecture to collections of designers to conversations about fashion to travel. There is inspiration everywhere—just be open to it.

Creating the time.

Q: How did you find the time for working on your business even with your day job? Do you work mornings before work? Evenings? Weekends?

Andre: I typically write on evenings and weekends.

Q: Did you give up anything else to spend more time on this?

Andre: I'm an outgoing person by nature, so I've

had to forgo some social occasions to write and research. It really comes down to discipline and consistency. I'd say these are two of the most valuable life skills I've learned that have benefited me.

Q: What habits did you need to put into place?

Andre: There are times when I don't feel like writing, but because I want to remain consistent, I write. I may not post everything I write, but the key is to write. Put the ideas down on paper and watch how things happen.

Q: How much time do you spend on your business?

Andre: I can't necessarily quantify how much time I spend on the business, but I'm always thinking about how I can grow and improve it. The trick is to perform your day job exceptionally while still pursuing your passion, and not to allow your day job to consume all your energy and time. Find balance.

Finding energy/mindset.

Q: Did you make any changes to your lifestyle to support your new business venture?

Andre: I didn't make any changes other than cutting back on some social activities so that I could write and post on a regular basis.

Q: What are tips you have for managing your time?

Andre: Establishing a regular day/time to write and post for your blog enables you to stay consistent.

Q: Do you advise others to try this if they are interested in fashion and personal consulting?

Andre: This business is about relationships as much as it is about the value you bring. You will need to meet as many people as you can to get the word out about what it is you do. However, you must balance this with making sure you are educating yourself and staying abreast of trends in order to prove your value.

Q: What is the single biggest change you had to make to support your business?

Andre: The biggest change I had to make was to become adept at social media, specifically Instagram. Understanding your audience and providing compelling content that engages is critical to success in this field. I meet with other fashion bloggers and stylists on a regular basis to exchange information and support for each other.

Q: Do you want to spend more time on your fashion business eventually? Or quit your day job and become totally dedicated to your business?

Andre: At some point, I'd like to pursue my passion full time. In the meantime, my goal is to continue to build a following, improve my writing, and network with others in the industry. What I've learned from others who are in this field is that you need a starting point. Whether it's a blog or social media presence, you'll need something tangible to launch your brand.

Dream Big with Cassandra Gaisford

"Your challenge - dream big. Everything starts as someone's daydream. Fuel your verve—pursue the vision that sparkles. Become audaciously obsessed. Dream big but plan small. Baby steps will lead to bigger success. Anchor your dreams within your heart and feel as though they are already achieved." - Cassandra Gaisford

I discovered author Cassandra Gaisford when I read her *Career Rescue* books. She writes inspiring non-fiction about how to live a creative life, pursue your passion, and make meaningful change in your life. A number one bestselling Amazon author, she also writes romance and historical fiction, and is a coach and speaker.

Cassandra is inspiring because she leads by example—she follows her passion for writing and art, and she helps others find their creativity through her entrepreneurial writing business, which includes coaching and speaking.

She is a fellow nine-to-five job escapee. Read on to learn about Cassandra. You'll find that she's an inspiring example of a person who found space in her life to create.

Finding the place.

Q: Where do you work on your business?

Cassandra: I run my business from home in a beautiful office overlooking the picturesque Bay of Islands, in Northland, New Zealand. I feel very fortunate to live and work in such an inspiring place. I also know fortune favors the bold! I've worked hard and made courageous and audacious decisions to get here.

I love variety. Sometimes I wander down to The Shed—an old building on the edge of our 10-acre property. Recently I've renamed it "the engagement room"—it's where I work on the things I love.

Q: Did you have to clean up/clear clutter first?

Cassandra: I'm a collector. Recently, I heard my partner tell someone that I collect anything related to positivity. In many of my books, I share that my deepest obsession is my passion for passion. My desk is often strewn with articles about passionate people, interesting things I have found and inspirational ideas that I'd like to work on later. This can lead to overwhelm at times, so I tend to favor clearing away distractions before working.

To stay inspired and ignite motivation, I love to place an inspiring book on my desk or an inspiring quote on my wall.

Currently, I have an open page from *The Art of Success: How Extraordinary Artists Can Help You Succeed in Business and Life,* which is inspired by Leonardo da Vinci. I choose a new page daily to guide me and help set the tone for the day.

While responding to your questions, I've closed the book and reopened it intuitively at the section

"Empower Your Spirit." I opened the page on the chapter *Worship the God Within*. This chapter reminds me how important spirituality and faith is to my creative practice—as it was to Leonardo, and is to so many other creative people, too.

One of my daily practices is to ensure I clear my desk at the end of the day, and write a few notes regarding the focus for the next day. I celebrate my successes by writing them in my journal and acknowledging the things I'm grateful for.

This creates joy and space in my mind, and enables me to approach the new day feeling inspired and focused—assuming I've also cleared my mind by meditating, completing my morning pages, and walking in the morning, too.

Q: How do you get inspired? Do you go anywhere to "fill your creative well?"

Cassandra: Inspiration is everywhere—movies, music, magazines, bookshops, online, in the garden. I can't think of anywhere or anything that can't be a source of inspiration. Even discordant things and situations can ignite a spark. One of my wise writing friends once encouraged me to channel upsetting personal situations into my books. Some of the scenes in my upcoming historical novel are my favorite because the emotion I poured into them is so intense. Nothing is wasted.

Recently, I began thinking deeply about the notion of duty as a writer, as a woman, as a person in this world at this time. And I realized how thankful I am to people who have shared their creative journey—the heartaches and the joys. I am tremendously inspired by people who have to battle to be true to themselves. And I decided I wanted to "pay it forward" by helping myself and others who dream of creative success.

I wanted to do this by writing more self-empowerment books—books in which I share my journey to prosperity and the significant challenges I've had to overcome to be true to my art.

I've done this in part in my *Art of Success* books. *The Prosperous Author: How to Make a Living With Your Writing* will be a more intimate look into my creative process and contain the success secrets that have helped me leave a job I hated to become a full-time author and creative entrepreneur, follow my passion and make a great living with my writing.

It's only recently I began to value my writing as my gift, and it's something I've struggled for over 50 years to prioritize.

Helping others also fills my creative well—I've heard this referred to as "the helpers high." It's a lovely addiction to have.

I'm a woman of pristine intuition, and I work to keep it that way. A regular spiritual practice, looking after my well-being, spending time in nature, meditating, a fascination with and deep respect for the nuances of other people lives—including their hobbies, interests, and obsessions—and yearly overseas trips are some of the many ways I get and stay inspired.

Doing "a combo" is fabulous, as I did recently when my partner and I went to Fiji for two weeks, combining many wellness strategies. We completely disconnected from social media, gave up alcohol, absorbed ourselves in local life, and nurtured our relationship.

Living a passionate life committed to creativity naturally feeds my inspiration.

My creative well was replenished when I moved away from my home of close to 50 years, Wellington, to The Bay of Islands. The climate, people, and pace of life here are a wonder tonic. I truly believe everyone has their soul space—the place that most feels like their spiritual home. Never give up searching for it.

I also love beautiful magazines—Urbis, Elle, Harper's Bazaar, Mindfood, and anything committed to beauty and stories of people living inspiring lives feed my creativity.

Other inspirational people are like vitamins for my soul. Sometimes I'll attend workshops like the one I did in Puglia, Italy, with photographer Carla Coulson. It was fabulous. I'll also chat on social media or engage their services. I guess you could say that these people are my mentors in some way.

In 2016 I invested a significant amount of time and money forging my new career direction as a creative entrepreneur. This included downscaling my coaching business and corporate work, signing up for courses and attending conferences to learn from experts in their fields.

A real highlight in 2016 was meeting Michael Hauge, a top Hollywood story expert, author, and lecturer who consults with writers, filmmakers, marketers, attorneys, and public speakers throughout the world. My goal was to have him sign one of my books, but I ended up building a very special friendship.

I'm also going to consult Michael again—especially for my big (secret) project that has already been suggested by a top literary agent could become a movie. I know paying for these services will fast-track my success and feed my goal to be the best writer I can. I consulted with him when writing one of my romance novels, *The Italian Billionaire's Christmas Bride*, and the feedback was invaluable.

Plus, I've signed up for a class with my guru Tim Ferris to boost my success and productivity further: *How Billionaires, Icons, and World-Class Performers Master Productivity*.

One of the investments I've also made is taking a fiction writing class with James Patterson. As of January 2016, James has sold over 350 million books worldwide and currently holds the Guinness World Record for the most #1 *New York Times* bestsellers. I'd love to achieve that kind of success!

Creating the time.

Q: How did you find the time for working on your business?

Cassandra: When I started my coaching business, I was a single mother with a mortgage, but I didn't let that stop me from chasing my dream. Being a single mum also fueled the desire, and the need, because I could never get enough leave to keep up with all my daughter's school holidays!

I worked nights and weekends at first. Then, when the money started to flow, I negotiated a four-day workweek. Not long after, as I began to feel more confident in my abilities to be self-employed AND pay my bills, I quit. It was a terrific day!

Along with other creatives, I share more about my journey to self-employment and include a chapter about how to finance your career on a shoestring in my book, *Mid-Life Career Rescue (Employ Yourself): How to Confidently Leave a Job You Hate, and Start Living a Life You Love, Before It's Too Late.*

Q: A theme of my book is giving up something else to live a creative life and go after what you want. Did you give up anything else to spend more time on the life you want to live?

Cassandra: I'm not a heavy drinker, but I was

drinking more than I wanted. I decided to take a break from alcohol in the lead up to Christmas 2016. I felt so great that in 2017 I decided to experiment with my commitment to be alcohol-free for the *whole* year. My partner decided to join me. Many people want to quit but struggle, as we did. I will share what I learned and what really works in my new book, *Your Beautiful Mind: Control Alcohol, Discover Freedom, Find Happiness and Change Your Life*.

Alcohol addiction remains a hidden and stigmatic problem marked by denial and fear. It's also an incredible time-waster, and damaging to your long-term creativity.

Other things that I did to allow more creativity in my life include:

-Selling my television.

-Downsizing my coaching business.

-Less socializing. "No" is a beautiful word. Plus, it helps that I'm no longer drinking, as so much socializing is built around alcohol.

-Stopping procrastination and making excuses.

-Checking emails and social media less. I only check in at 12 pm and 4 pm with emails, and then for only 15-30 minutes, scanning for priorities.

-Stopping hiding my spirituality and fearing that people might think I was spooky when I talked about my love and use of tarot, oracles, Reiki, energy work, and mediums. A turning point was when a client accused me of witchcraft when I suggested she try lavender essential oil to alleviate some of her stress.

These techniques and others were good enough for Coco Chanel, and good enough for me! And I've been rewarded—so many people have sought me out because of the spiritual and creative side I bring, combined with strong business skills.

I also gave up doing projects that are easy and neglecting passion projects that sometimes are beyond my current level of expertise, but that would challenge me and enable me to grow, and would provide greater fulfillment.

I quit short working days and two or three-day weekends. I want to work longer— but I still am mindful of balance, which is why I am careful to take time out during the day to reconnect with those around me, even if I choose to make up the hours on the other end. I gave up saying, "I have to." I replaced this with "I choose to"—for this is a greater truth.

I gave up the comfort rut of certainty. I bought myself three months to finish my historical art-related novel. This is the novel I pitched to a top literary agent and also to Penguin Publishing over seven years ago. It's the book I told myself I could never write. Both expressed an eagerness to see the finished book.

There is no certainty of a contract. There is no certainty that my book will sell or in any way repay my investment. There is only the certainty that I shall not die with regret, wondering "What if?"

I have given up waiting for the timing to be right. I have given up waiting for excess money. I've given up living without discomfort and taking on work that pays well but that I don't enjoy in the hope that I will make money I can store away for that "rainy day" when the conditions are "perfect to write my book."

The greatest comfort of all is being true to yourself, to the passionate stirrings of your soul. For that reason, I decided to invest in myself this year. I have given myself the luxury of time. I decided to bankroll three months out of the world. You could say I bankrolled the space to complete what many people have told me will be my greatest work. We'll see.

Q: How much time do you spend on your business? What habits did you need to put in place?

Cassandra: I love what I do, so like the author James Patterson, working seven days doesn't feel like a slog to me. It's a joy, a privilege; it's play. I also like his comment, "Do NOT sit there like 'Oh I don't feel like it today. I don't feel like it tomorrow.' Feel like it! Do it! Force yourself."

But keeping balance, and knowing as I do that without a commitment to health and well-being it's easy to burn out and be inefficient, I'll be keeping an eye on outcomes versus hours spent. And I'll be investing in smart daily habits like meditation, yoga, eating well, etc.

New habits also include greater discipline to maintain focus and eliminate all distractions when I write. I've developed a new habit that I love—writing in 30-minute cycles. Using the timer helps keep me honest.

Right now, one of my favorite tools for this is focusatwill.com. The developers say this will work magic because it's "scientifically optimized music to help you focus." I'm a big fan. I love the music, and love what it's doing for my productivity. It is incredible how much you can achieve in 30-minute bursts when you are focused.

I gave up watching TV over five years ago. This has been life changing. It's such a time-zapper, and most times depressing.

Health is a priority. I'm halfway to my next life. I want to make sure I arrive in good shape. Alcohol is gone. Coffee too. Sugar is on the way out. Coming in: green and clean and raw. Meditation needs to be more regular for sure. I've been a meditator for over 20 years, but sometimes I forget to prioritize it.

I'm going to get up earlier. at 5:00 am, and "just do it!" This is going to be challenging, but I'm determined to make this a joyful ritual.

My writing rituals will include five nine-hour days per week dedicated to fiction, one day for nonfiction and working with coaching clients and marketing/business activities. Day seven will be a passion day—whatever I decide that will be.

Included in these commitments is prioritizing balance—relationships, health, and spiritual. Meditation, romance, chilling will all factor in—including a reward trip to Japan with my partner in September to defrag and re-top up our inspiration well.

Finding the energy/mindset.

Q: Did you make any changes to your lifestyle to

support your new business venture?

Cassandra: Mindset and managing energy is EVERYTHING.

Meditate, eat well, exercise regularly, and make room for rest to keep energy levels high. Don't take any devices into your bedroom at night—including your phone. Only read paperback books at night (for relaxation)—not work-related research. Switch off to switch on. No working after 10:00 pm—it's hard to sleep if you're all fired up and inspired.

Move. I force myself to get out and walk every day. It helps when I remind myself how many para-plegics would love to be able to stand on their legs and go for a stroll.

Last year I purchased a standing desk, which also lowers to be a normal workstation. I love the option to stand or sit.

I purchased Dragon software to use dictation to write, and GhostReader to check errors and improve flow by using this technology to read my work back out loud. I also use Scrivener to help me structure my thoughts and writing, and have greater control over my production and outputs. It's wonderful to be in control of my publishing success.

But this has meant dedicating time to learning new technology—but once again, you need to invest in efficient systems and processes to reap the rewards.

Other great strategies to boost a positive, focused mindset: I keep a praise file—record and look at the feedback people give you regularly. I started 15 years ago—originally to help me overcome acute self-doubt. But now, while I need it less, it is affirming and heart-stirring to read the unsolicited feedback others have said. And sometimes when people, family included, say something hostile about my work (like my brother, who said, "Great, just what we all need—more advice from you"), knowing I have touched someone's life and made the world a better place reminds me of what gives my life meaning and purpose. It makes the tougher times worthwhile.

I'm a big fan of creating a passion journal every

year—this keeps my mind on what I want to create, and empowers my ability to manifest by leveraging off the laws of intention, attraction, and desire. I have a free gift for your readers, a passion journal workbook for those who subscribe to my newsletter at www.cassandraGaisford.com.

Q: Any tips for managing your time?

Cassandra: 30-minute bursts of activity are amazing for getting into a productive mindset.

Be strong with others who want to zap your time. Push back and check if their demands on your time are urgent. "No" is a beautiful word.

Be a creative procrastinator—put off until tomorrow things that don't enable you to achieve progress toward your goals today.

Combine tasks. I listen to audio books while walking, podcasts while preparing meals or doing chores or when I am at the supermarket. This helps prevent resentment when I attend to some of the more mundane things that "take me away" from writing or perfecting my craft.

Delegate and outsource. In our Kiwi culture, we have a "do it yourself" mentality. In the past, I tried to do it all, but have found it way more efficient to hand things to the pros. It didn't always cost me more money, and when it did, I often recouped it in increased sales—like great cover design or the improved professionalism of having a passionate proofreader look over my books. I've been fortunate to meet many skilled people who have read my career rescue books, including a lady who was inspired to quit her job and has started an editing business. I now outsource some of my work to her.

Q: What are some of the things you tell your clients if they want to make a change and lead more creative lives?

Cassandra: Prioritize your creativity. It's that simple—but at times, that is challenging. Isolate the barriers, blocks, whatever is standing in the way.

148

Take an inventory and then commit to problem solving. Intensify your desire, remind yourself of your "why." What benefits will flow? How will you feel if you never try?

Be inspired by other people who have made the leap to creativity. Read their stories— people like Coco Chanel, Leonardo da Vinci, Frida Kahlo, and so many others. I can't think of one successful person who hasn't had to fight for their dream. Conflict and overcoming obstacles in the norm—but it's also what makes for compelling viewing and dedicated fans.

Do it scared—most of the successful creative people I know started and continued to create despite their doubts, fears, and anxieties. Follow your passion to prosperity!

Q: What is the single biggest change you had to make to support your business?

Cassandra: Invest in myself. As one of my creative clients sagely said, "You have to bankroll your dreams. In the beginning, the money isn't there." I go into how to finance your career (on a shoestring) in a big way in my book *Mid-Life Career Rescue (Employ Yourself): How to Confidently Leave a Job You Hate and Start Living a Life You Love Before It's Too Late*.

I've also committed to a daily practice of feeding optimism, and aligning my thoughts with the outcome I desire, not fear. This has been a key part of my success, and continues to be—but it's not something that comes naturally. This may surprise people, but I also believe it is true of many creatives.

And, as I said before, as I stopped waiting for inspiration and I showed up every day to do The Work, my muse began to take me seriously, and now she shows up too.

Find Cassandra Gaisford online, learn about her books, and read her blog: www.cassandragaisford.com and on her Amazon page: amazon.com/author/cassandragaisford

Rolling Like Mike, Skeeball Entrepreneur

"It all about the communitskee. It doesn't matter whether or not you are good at skeeball. If you come in with an open mind and a willingness to make new friends, you're going to have a ball."

-Mike Fraser, Skee-EO, The Skee League

Whether you're looking for a unique team-building activity for your next corporate outing or want a new sports league to join, Mike Fraser is your go-to guy in Chicago.

Mike runs the Skee League in Chicago. Remember skeeball machines from your childhood arcade days? The game is back and growing in popularity for adults as organized skeeball leagues have been popping up in cities around the U.S. for several years.

I met Mike, the Skee-EO, when I started playing in the league six years ago. Through skeeball, I've met and bonded with some of my closest friends. My team made it to the playoffs a few times, but lost a lot, too. We still had fun no matter the outcome.

The competition can be intense, but Mike has always made the league friendly and warm. He has a knack for remembering the names of all 180 people playing in the league during a given season, and also creates a custom nickname for each player.

I chose to feature Mike as a case study because I want to show you it's possible to turn a unique, niche interest into a full-time business. Mike is one of the best examples of someone who has followed an entrepreneurial path and overcome obstacles to achieve success.

Recently, I asked Mike how skeeball came into his life. Here are Mike's thoughts, in his words, to this and other questions.

Q: How did you get started with skeeball?

Mike: I wish I could tell you I was a childhood

skeeball prodigy, and that starting my leagues had always been a lifelong dream, but the truth is, it was
more of a happy accident. Or should I say "happskee
accskeedent." (You have probably already noticed:
We use a lot of puns.)

I had just gotten laid off from a corporate sales
job selling advertising for print and online yellow
pages. The yellow page industry was in a steep de-
cline, and to say corporate life had left a bitter taste
in my mouth would be a massive understatement.

I wanted to pursue something where I was in
complete control of the customer experience, so I began doing online marketing for a few existing clients
under my own LLC. Knowing I needed side income,
a friend of mine from high school suggested I get the
ball rolling on a skeeball league here in Chicago. He
had played in college and had a lot of fun, so I figured, why not?

It took a lot of work in the beginning, but once
we found our following, the league garnered some
publicity and took off. Fortunately, I was able to fold

it all into my existing company.

Finding the place.

Q: Where do you work on your business? Do you have an office somewhere or work from home?

Mike: That's a funny question that rarely gets asked! I split my time working from an attorney's office and squatting at local coffee shops. The attorney was actually a client from my advertising days above, but now we are more friends than anything. I still help him out where I can, but my purpose is more along the lines of office companionship. We are more productive together than we would be alone. Wherever I am, I drink a ton of coffee.

Q: Did you go through a time when you still worked a day job and worked your business on the side?

Mike: No, I've never done another main nine-to-five job. I've been tempted, I just never found the right fit that would still allow me the necessary time and space to continue to grow and expand my own business. Instead, I've piled on lots of other side jobs. I still do the online marketing/consulting for small to medium-sized businesses, coach kids' recess at an elementary school, bartend, and am a rideshare driver for Lyft.com. I've got a lot of different balls in the air. (ZING!)

Q: Did you have to clean up/clear clutter first?

Mike: I am the clutter. I'm not comfortable in an area until I've spread all my belongings around so I can see them. You can tell where I've been working because it looks like a tornado has come through. I make really organized people's skin crawl. It's symptomatic of having a "monkey-mind."

Q: Do you ever work in a cafe or library?

Mike: I LOVE working at cafés. I feed off the energy of the crowd and the "white noise" effect of a cacophony of conversations. It's a great environment to hammer out busy work, routine tasks, or even case studies for best-selling books.

On the flip side, I love libraries for the exact opposite reason. When I'm brainstorming or trying to think creatively, I need complete quiet. I like to shut my eyes and put my head down on the table to concentrate. It's weird, but it works for me!

Q: How do you get inspired? Do you go anywhere to "fill your creative well?"

Mike: I'm on the go a lot, so podcasts are the absolute best. I'm really into "How I Built This" at the moment. It's just real stories of entrepreneurs sharing their experiences and the winding road they took to overcome failures and build extremely successful businesses. If I could bottle the energy I feel after listening to one and sell it, I'd be filthy rich. "Start Up" and "Ted Radio Hour" are also worth checking out.

Creating the time.

Q: How did you find the time for working on your business?

Mike: I'm a procrastinator by nature, but never miss a deadline. If I say I'm going to do something, I get it done. Accountability is a virtue I do not take lightly. I make time to get whatever it is I need to get done. This can result in days where I'm less productive followed by long binges of work sessions. The trade off is there isn't really much difference in the week. Meaning, I don't (usually) take the weekend "off." I'm always doing something. My fiancé finds it annoying, but that's the life of an entrepreneur.

Q: A theme of my book is giving up something else to live a creative life and go after what you want. Did you give up anything else to spend more time on the life you want to live?

Mike: Aside from the obvious—making less money—you never realize how important health benefits are until you find yourself outside the comfortable umbrella of corporate health insurance. Being self-employed meant paying out the wazoo for plans that could only be described as "garbage" in comparison to my previous employer's plan. I'm a leukemia survivor, so because of my pre-existing condition I was fortunate enough to get covered for insurance through the Affordable Care Act, but it certainly pales in comparison to being in a group plan. Now that Donald Trump is president, who knows what I'm going to do?

Q: How much time do you spend on your business? What habits did you need to put in place?

Mike: I don't have any set time allotment. I wake up, and I do as much as I can possibly do on that day. Then, when I feel like I need to rest, I rest. I might feel rested and rise at 2:00 am and get some work done. I don't work on a strict schedule. I listen to my body and mind as a guide. When you are working on your own business, work isn't a chore. It's just something that requires energy. I tend to pull some crazy hours, sometimes working from 8:00 am to 2:00 am when leagues are in session. Hence, the coffee. It definitely can cause an imbalance, if you're not careful.

Finding the energy/mindset.

Q: Did you make any changes to your lifestyle to support your new business venture? For example, did you change anything about your sleep habits, eating, or workout habits?

Mike: I go to bed *way* earlier than I ever used to. I used to always stay up past midnight; now it's more like 10:00 pm. Not sure if that was a conscious business decision or just the fact I'm getting old. Probably the latter. I still have to suck it up and stay out late during league nights, but it's getting more and more painful.

I still don't eat as healthy as I should, but I have made the conscious decision to keep some healthy snacks in my car. Since I sometimes go without eating dinner while working during league nights, the only available options while I'm driving home after 1:00 am are McDonald's or White Castle. That's a lose/lose situation.

The most significant lifestyle change was when I stopped drinking alcohol four years ago. People are amazed, since I spend so much time in bars, but it was something that was necessary for me to run my business like a professional. Probably the best decision I've ever made, not just for business, but also for life.

Q: What are some of the things you tell others if they want to make a change and lead a more creative life?

Mike: Get connected with larger groups of people who are already doing or interested in doing what you want to do. Learn as much as you can. Build relationships. Leaps of faith are really scary, but it helps to have people on the journey with you along the way to help you stay up or cushion the fall when you hit some inevitable bumps in the road.

Q: What is the single biggest change you had to make to support your business?

Mike: I had to learn how to get really good at skeeball! I was terrible when I first started the league. It really is a game that requires time and repetition. I wouldn't say I'm the best roller in the league, but after five years and three perfect 900 games, I consider myself one of the top skeeballers in Chicago! #SKEEGOALS #THESKEELEAGUE #HUNDO-BALL

Find out more about the Skee League by visiting: theskeeleague.com.

Conclusion

"Success is an inside job. Put yourself together, and your world falls into place."

-Gary Keller

I hope you found the interviews with Andre, Cassandra, and Mike inspiring. While each approach their businesses slightly differently, they all have something in common—**they made space in their lives to pursue what matters to them**.

• Andre devoted his weekends and evenings to starting his personal styling business. It doesn't feel like work because passion fuels him.

• Cassandra changed her business model, moved across the country, prioritized purposeful joy, and adopted a healthier lifestyle. She is a prolific writer and driven to create.

• Mike made space in his life for learning and energizing himself with entrepreneurial podcasts, and by giving up alcohol to focus on his health and business.

I hope my message—that creativity can bring more happiness to your life—is clear. So far in my journey, giving up negative ways of thinking to focus on positive routines and affirmations has opened up a new, more creative career path.

How will you live a more creative life? You don't have to become a full-time artist to gain the benefits of creativity; you simply need to open your mind to new experiences.

You can take the following small actions that will lead to big change.

Create Space.

- Declutter and create a clean, minimal space where you can think, dream, and create.
- Novelty can stimulate our creativity. Consider finding new spaces to work (cafes, libraries, the outdoors).
- Remove obstacles to creativity. Delegate, negotiate or eliminate non-value added tasks.

Find Time.

- Spend fifteen minutes every morning on a new project that will spark your creativity.
- If you don't have a project yet, spend the time writing your thoughts and observations in a journal. Trust in the process of emergence

and allow creativity to grow.

Manage Your Energy.

- Start a morning routine where the first thing you do is focus on your creativity. Do this long enough and you will build a creativity habit.
- Go to bed fifteen minutes earlier each night.
- Tape a note on your wall that says, "I am growth-minded. I am learning every day. I embrace challenges and seek to grow." Say it out loud every morning.

In *Groundhog Day*, the writers asked an underlying question, "How do you want to live your life?" Phil Connors was so jaded, they made him relive the same day over and over until the message was clear.

I challenge you with that same question and ask, "*Starting today*, how do you want to live your life?"

Make time for yourself today. Start small. Experiment. Try new things, and most importantly, live fully.

BONUS: 22 Books for Your Creative Journey

Companion Workbook and Free eBook: 21 Creativity Hacks

Claim your free bonus books here: projectmanagerwriter.com/thrivebonus.

Recommended Books

Many books have helped me on my journey to live a more creative life. I hope these recommendations help you in some way.

On Life

• Chasing Daylight: How My Forthcoming Death Transformed My Life – Eugene O'Kelly

• The Top Five Regrets of the Dying – Bronnie Ware

Creativity and Passion

- Big Magic – Elizabeth Gilbert
- The War of Art – Steven Pressfield
- How to Find Your Passion and Purpose: Four Easy Steps to Discover a Job You Want And Live the Life You Love - Cassandra Gaisford
- The Artist's Way – Julia Cameron
- The Creative Habit: Learn It and Use It for Life – Twyla Tharp

Entrepreneurship and Career Change

- The Four-Hour Work Week. Escape the 9-5, Live Anywhere and Join the New Rich – Tim Ferriss
- Tools of Titans: The Tactics, Routines, and Habits of Billionaires, Icons, and World-Class Performers - Tim Ferriss
- Career Change: Stop hating your job, discover what you really want to do with your life, and start

doing it! – Joanna Penn

- Mid-Life Career Rescue (Employ Yourself): How to change careers, confidently leave a job you hate, and start living a life you love, before it's too late – Cassandra Gaisford

Writing

- On Writing – Stephen King
- Bird by Bird: Some Instructions on Writing and Life – Anne Lamott
- The Successful Author Mindset: A Handbook for Surviving the Writer's Journey – Joanna Penn
- Prosperity for Writers: A Writer's Guide to Creating Abundance – Honoree Corder

Productivity and Success

- 15 Secrets Successful People Know About Time

Management: The Productivity Habits of 7 Billion-aires, 13 Olympic Athletes, 29 Straight-A Students, and 239 Entrepreneurs – Kevin Kruse

• The ONE Thing: The Surprisingly Simple Truth Behind Extraordinary Results – Gary Keller

• The Art of Success: Coco Chanel: How Extraor-dinary Artists Can Help You Succeed in Business and Life - Cassandra Gaisford

• How to Fail at Almost Everything and Still Win Big: Kind of the Story of My Life – Scott Adams

Psychology

• Mindset: The New Psychology of Success – Carol Dweck

• Drive: The Surprising Truth About What Moti-vates Us – Daniel Pink

• Flow: The Psychology of Optimal Experience - Mihaly Csikszentmihaly

References

Sources for data used in this book include the following studies and articles:

Jobs

- Guy Berger, "Will This Year's College Grads Job-Hop More Than Previous Grads?" LinkedIn, April 12, 2016.

- Lauren Weber, "Job Satisfaction Hits a 10-Year High—But It's Still Below 50%," The Wall Street Journal, July 19, 2016.

- Annamarie Mann and Jim Harter, "The Worldwide Employee Engagement Crisis," Gallup, January 7, 2016.

Happiness and Creativity

- Melissa Dahl, "A Classic Psychology Study on

Why Winning the Lottery Won't Make You Happier," New York Magazine, January 13, 2016.

• Daniel Kahneman and Angus Deaton, "High income improves evaluation of life but not emotional well-being," Center for Health and Well-being, Princeton University, August 4, 2010.

• B. J. Shannon, R. A. Dosenbach, Y. Su, A. G. Vlassenko, L. J. Larson-Prior, T. S. Nolan, A. Z. Snyder, M. E. Raichle, "Morning-evening variation in human brain metabolism and memory circuits," Journal of Neurophysiology, March 1, 2013.

• Nicole Brown, "$83,000 Is The New $75,000 Happiness Benchmark For Annual Income," Social Media Week, January 22, 2015.

• Alex Lickerman M.D., "How to Reset Your Happiness Set Point," Psychology Today, April 21, 2013.

• Zak Stambor, "Is our happiness set in stone?" American Psychological Association, December 2007.

• Silvia, Paul J.; Beaty, Roger E.; Nusbaum, Emily

C.; Eddington, Kari M.; Levin-Aspenson, Holly; Kwapil, Thomas R., "Everyday creativity in daily life: An experience-sampling study of "little c" creativity," Psychology of Aesthetics, Creativity, and the Arts, May 2014.

• Linda Naiman, "Want Happier, More Productive Employees? Invest More in Creativity and Design," Inc.com, November 21, 2016.

Social Media and Media

• Against All Odds Productions, Inc. and Luminous Content, "The Human Face of Big Data," PBS.org, re-aired June 2016.

• Delvv, "Survey Reveals U.S. Adults Are Bombarded With Irrelevant Information On Their Smartphones," PR Newswire, August 18, 2015.

• Caitlin Johnson, "Cutting Through Advertising Clutter," CBSNews.com, September 17, 2006.

Habits and Wellness

- Phillippa Lally, Cornelia H. M. van Jaarsveld, Henry W. W. Potts, and Jane Wardle, "How are habits formed: Modelling habit formation in the real world," European Journal of Social Psychology, July 16, 2009.

- California Energy Commission, "Windows and Offices: A Study of Office Worker Performance and the Indoor Environment," www.energy.ca.gov, October 2003.

Take Action Today...

DOWNLOAD YOUR FREE BONUSES

Download the workbook and your free eBook: *21 Creativity Hacks: A To-Do List for Your Inner Creative*. Start your creative reboot today by heading to: projectmanagerwriter.com/thrivebonus.

SIGN UP FOR MY NEWSLETTER

Join my growing community of readers! When you sign up, you'll receive monthly updates about productivity tools and tips to help creatives like you reach your goals. By downloading the workbook, you'll automatically be subscribed. You can also visit ProjectManagerWriter.com to sign up and receive a free eBook.

JOIN ME ON FACEBOOK

Join my readers on www.facebook.com/Court-Kennwrite. Let us know what you think of this book, the workbook, and *21 Creativity Hacks*. What do you want to learn about creativity and productivity?

Thank You

Thank you for joining me in this journey to find space for your creativity! If you found this book useful, I'd really appreciate a review. Reviews help new readers discover my books and are greatly appreciated.

Thank you!
Courtney Kenney
ProjectManagerWriter

Want to learn how to become a more productive and prosperous author? Get your free eBook, *The Productive Author Roadmap,* at projectmanagerwriter.com.

About the Author

Courtney Kenney is an author and book launch consultant. She spent 16 years working as a project manager at technology companies. She left corporate life behind and is now a freelance project manager and runs her own author business.

Courtney helps entrepreneurs launch bestselling books and grow their author platforms. She lives in Chicago with her husband and loves walking, exploring new neighborhoods, traveling, and playing in a competitive skeeball league.

Visit her website, projectmanagerwriter.com, where she writes about becoming a more productive and prosperous author. Get her free ebook, *Productive Author Roadmap: Write More, Streamline Your Publishing, Simplify Your Marketing, and Adopt a Productive Author Mindset*.

Connect with Courtney online:

Projectmanagerwriter.com/contact

Twitter.com/pmpwriter

Facebook.com/courtkennwrite

Instagram/authorunleashed

More books by Courtney Kenney:

Layoff Reboot: Bounce Back from Job Loss and Find a Career You Love

Unleash Your Author: Write a Book in 30 Days

7-Step Book Launch Plan: Strategies to Publish and Promote Your Book

Copyright

Made in the USA
Monee, IL
30 December 2020